# MAKING CHANGES

# THE CYCLE OF CHANGE

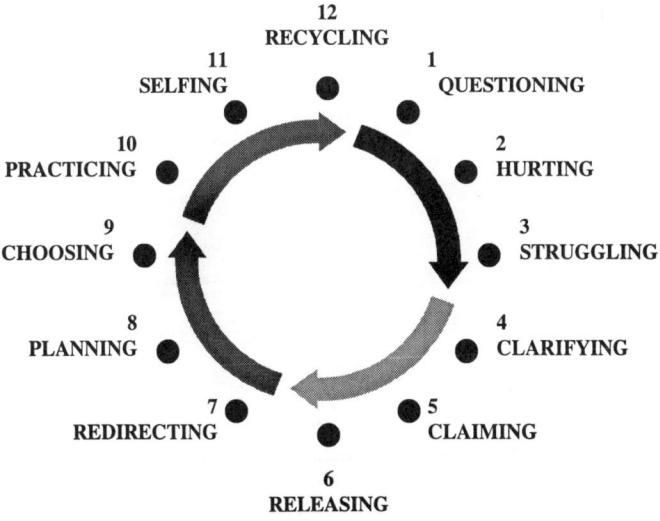

# Making

*A Guide Book for*

# Changes

*Managing Life's Challenges*

# J. Colleen Breen

Deaconess Press
Minneapolis

MAKING CHANGES: A GUIDEBOOK FOR MANAGING LIFE'S CHALLENGES © 1995 by Deaconess Press. All rights reserved. No part of this publication may be used or reproduced in any manner whatsoever without written permission, except in the case of brief quotations embodied in critical articles and reviews. For further information, please contact the publisher.

Published by Deaconess Press, 2450 Riverside Avenue South, Minneapolis, MN 55454.

**Library of Congress Cataloging-in-Publication Data**

Making changes : a guidebook for managing life's challenges
        p.    cm.
    ISBN 0-925190-33-0 : $12.95
    1. Life change events--Psychological aspects    2. Life change events--Case studies.   3. Adjustment (Psychology)--Case studies 4. Cognitive therapy    I. Title.
    BF637.L53B745  1994
    158'.1--dc20
    [B]                                               94-41717
                                                              CIP

First printing: December 1994

Printed in the United States of America
99  98  97  96  95            7  6  5  4  3  2  1

Cover design by the Nancekivell Group

Publisher's Note: Deaconess Press publishes books and other materials related to the subjects of physical health, mental health, and chemical dependency. Its publications, including *Making Changes*, do not necessarily reflect the philosophy of Fairview Hospital and Healthcare Services or their treatment programs

*In loving memory of my father, Maurice T. Breen, who taught me the usefulness of maps and who never let anyone be a stranger very long.*

# CONTENTS

INTRODUCTION . . . . . . . . . . . . . . . . . . . . . . . . . . . . . . . . .  1

ACKNOWLEDGING

    CHAPTER 1: QUESTIONING . . . . . . . . . . . . . . . . . . . . .  7

    CHAPTER 2: HURTING . . . . . . . . . . . . . . . . . . . . . . . . .  23

    CHAPTER 3: STRUGGLING . . . . . . . . . . . . . . . . . . . . . .  39

    CHAPTER 4: CLARIFYING . . . . . . . . . . . . . . . . . . . . . . .  57

ACCEPTING

    CHAPTER 5: CLAIMING . . . . . . . . . . . . . . . . . . . . . . . . .  71

    CHAPTER 6: RELEASING . . . . . . . . . . . . . . . . . . . . . . . .  83

    CHAPTER 7: REDIRECTING . . . . . . . . . . . . . . . . . . . . . .  97

    CHAPTER 8: PLANNING . . . . . . . . . . . . . . . . . . . . . . . .  111

ACCOMMODATING

    CHAPTER 9: CHOOSING . . . . . . . . . . . . . . . . . . . . . . . .  127

    CHAPTER 10: PRACTICING . . . . . . . . . . . . . . . . . . . . . .  139

    CHAPTER 11: SELFING . . . . . . . . . . . . . . . . . . . . . . . . .  153

RECYCLING

    CHAPTER 12: RECYCLING . . . . . . . . . . . . . . . . . . . . . .  163

CONCLUSION . . . . . . . . . . . . . . . . . . . . . . . . . . . . . . . . .  173

# INTRODUCTION

*C*hange is just the way things are. Our options and choices lie in how to change.

*Making Changes* is a book about how to change. An early working title, *How Do You Learn What You Need To Know For The Journey You Hadn't Planned to Take?* captured the process part of the business of change. But this book also addresses pain, another unavoidable part of life and change.

In my opinion, there are two kinds of pain: necessary and optional. This book describes how to distinguish between the two and offers strategies for reducing the stress of change resulting from optional suffering.

*Making Changes* describes a one-size-fits-all model for planned personal change. This model presents an integrated and holistic approach to change which includes the whole person: mind, body, and soul. Soul is not easy to talk about, especially in the context of therapeutic problem solving. Yet we are mind/body/spirit beings. Leaving out one part would be like trying to divide a bubble.

While formally trained in Gestalt and interpersonal therapies, I have found Cognitive Behavioral Therapy (CBT) theory and methods useful and adaptable to my work. However, I find traditional CBT to be underdeveloped and lacking in some important ways. Like other traditional therapies, it does not address soul matters. I've found this is where people often get stuck, for deep beliefs about who we are and how we view our lives are connected to soul.

Through my work in pastoral counseling and spiritual development in the 1960s and 70s, I was privileged to work intimately with thousands of people in the midst of difficult and painful life changes. The education and experience I received doing this work helped me understand the importance of soul in change.

For the past ten years I have continued to develop and practice my hybrid version of CBT at the Stress and Depression Management Center at Riverside Medical Center in Minneapolis, Minnesota. Working in both inpatient hospital and outpatient clinic settings, I developed the cycle of change as a map for moving through the change process. This map helps clients revive their drooping spirits and make a do-able, pragmatic plan for change. It considers the whole self and it promotes self-counseling tools, which integrate traditional and personal styles. In 1988, I created Breen InnerPrizes to expand the application of the cycle of change to consulting and training with school districts, businesses, and industries undergoing accelerated, unwanted change in the marketplace. It worked there, too, according to the visible and audible "Ah-ha!"s of participants outside the therapeutic mileau.

In my professional work and life, I have come to know that change is not an option. Change is life work, and it is hard. There are many ways to get tripped up; not everyone starts at the same place, and we do not all get stuck in the same way. Some of us try to solve the wrong problem, like when we try to deny the aging process or try to have it all. Others try to solve what's not solvable, like trying to have relationships without pain, trying to live in the past, or trying to change someone else. These and other misguided efforts result in tense bodies, agitated minds, and weary spirits.

The model presented here, the cycle of change, has been developed with and used by women and men suffering from stress, depression, anxiety, and other problems related to the reality of impermanence. The purpose of this book is to assist you in reducing the stress of change by helping you develop tools and skills to use with the activities of change. These are condensed in this brief AAA "recipe" for how to change:

1. Acknowledge what is.
2. Accept what might be.
3. Accommodate to what will be.

Self-love is important for dealing with change, and it is a soul matter. Early in life, we are impressed with central messages about ourselves and the world. These are related to major themes: acceptance, belonging, control, and competence. When beliefs are inaccurate or debilitating, when we hook "OKness" as a person to these skewed conditions, self-equilibrium is disrupted.

We are often driven by inaccurate beliefs abbreviated into emotional thought-bytes such as: earn love, be perfect, be strong, do everything. The more these beliefs become habitual, the more powerful and harder to change they become. This is because beliefs are value-laden thoughts connected to soul.

In *Making Changes*, I profile three individuals' true life stories to illustrate real dilemmas with the process of change. In some examples we can observe techniques and skill-building tools in action. I hope you will look at these situations and consider those in your own life.

Above all, *Making Changes* is a guidebook on how to change. It's laced with the principles of cognitive behavioral therapy, but also includes matters of the soul. It is a reasonable approach to using your mind for a change, offering coaching in this pursuit.

This book is for people wanting a clearer picture, or map, for the overview of change, which can be described as the cycle of having/losing/having again. It is a book for anyone wanting to make changes more easily and less stressfully, and for those who tend to repeat the same mistakes. It is for those who get entangled with confusing emotions and faulty reasoning, and those who think in terms of inaccurate beliefs which lead to perplexing detours. *Making Changes* is for those of us who ask the wrong questions and don't know we're doing it, and for people of us who are serious about maneuvering through change in a way that will weave what works into our lives and weed out what doesn't.

Self is the fundamental agent of change. If we are not in charge of our selves, who is? Who directs our mental, physical, and emotional energies? The challenge of change is using your self—all of who you are—and dealing with what life hands you.

Living as the bosses of our selves takes daring, risk, and openness to adventure. And we can always count on an adventure to hold a few surprises for us.

# Acknowledging

# 1
## QUESTIONING

*Daring as it is to investigate the unknown, even more so it is to question the known.*
—Kaspar

Even though she married late in life, Marie looked forward to spending her retirement with her husband, enjoying their two sons and their hoped-for grandchildren. Unfortunately, within six short years she lost her husband to cancer and her younger son to Marfan's disease. At the time, Marie was a seventy-year-old retired social worker.

Debbie was a college professor married to a physician, and the mother of two children. She lived a lifestyle many young women choose to emulate: that of a woman who has it all. However, looks can be deceiving. For several years she had lived with the awareness that she was affectionately attracted to women. She put this knowledge on the back burner of her consciousness and hoped it would stay there. At age *thirty-four, Debbie fell in love with a coworker and realized that she must come to terms with her affection for women.*

*Larry, a forty-eight-year-old middle manager for a major food processor, started as a kitchen aide in research and development right out of high school. He enjoyed his work, and compared his feelings of loyalty for the corporation to those he held for his family. When the corporation was bought out and began restructuring, Larry was given the choice of being laid off or accepting a job demotion.*

The life circumstances of these three people are very different. However, the elements of their change processes are very much the same. All began the process by questioning the pain they were experiencing.

## Questioning Pain

I am a *cognitive behavioral* therapist working with adults who are struggling with significant stress. No one comes to me saying, "I feel just fine, thank you," or "Everything's great!" My clients come to me because they are angry, fearful, confused, sad, and worn out by struggle. Many are at or near the end of their ropes.

I have dedicated my therapy practice to providing clients the tools and training to become self-counselors. They become able to repair relationships broken by changes in their lifestyles. The client and I explore how he or she perceives the changing life situation that causes stress. We work together to repair the affected relationships with self, family, lovers, colleagues, employers, perpetrators, and even God. We start by exploring the pain.

Marie, who was struggling through the loss of loved ones, had questions about the pain she suffered that have been asked—and never adequately answered—by the human family since the first death of a human being. How can I go on alone? she wondered. "Could I have prevented this?" she asked.

Debbie's pain started as an internal dissatisfaction with her marriage and a feeling of incompleteness. The pain intensified when her attraction for women deepened into love for her coworker. She asked, "What do I do now? Do I act on my feelings at the cost of my ten-year marriage?"

Larry, displaced by the economic forces of a faceless marketplace and terrified by the possibility of long-term unemployment, asked, "How can this be when I've given it all I've got?"

There are two kinds of questioning: helpful and unhelpful. Why me? is a familiar unhelpful question—it doesn't lead to remedies or strategies. We need to cultivate helpful questions that give us information we can use.

Greek philosopher Heraclitus, known for his philosophy of universal change, described the world with this observation: "You cannot step into the same river twice; for fresh waters are ever flowing in upon you." It is possible that even in Heraclitus' time, 540-470 BC, this observation was hardly new. Although he may have tried to put a better spin on the idea by adding the soothing image of fresh waters, the truth is that all change—even change for the better—means loss. And loss causes pain.

There are two kinds of pain: necessary and optional. When we question our pain, we must first acknowledge that we all participate in a natural cycle of change known as life-death-rebirth. We see this fundamental cycle occurring throughout our lives as having-losing-having again. Painful changes happen in all our lives. They are an unavoidable part of being human.

Necessary suffering springs from our experience of change; it is a process of attaching and separating. Take, for example, a natural process with which we are all familiar—aging. We experience many physical, emotional, and spiritual changes during that process. We come to accept wearing bifocals, having a root canal, losing our hair, and losing muscle tone, even when the experience of those changes may be painful. Those physical changes conform to a gradual and predictable sequence of events we can see occurring in other people around us, as when parents see their children growing taller. They are evident in the nature of all things. We are prepared. We see those changes as inevitable.

Optional suffering is rooted in our perception of experience. Optional suffering doesn't need to be. It is pain of our own making. Imagine yourself lying in bed shivering while extra blankets are stashed in the closet a few steps away. You repeatedly say to yourself, I should get up and get another blanket. Whether you stay in your chilly bed or dash across your cold room to get a blanket, you understand that the choice is yours to make. You weigh how uncomfortable you are in bed against how uncomfortable you will be out of bed.

As you imagine this scene, you are probably deciding what you would do. Even if you recall an experience of a similar situation to determine your future response, you base your decision on your perception of yourself, your abilities, and your needs. Optional suf-

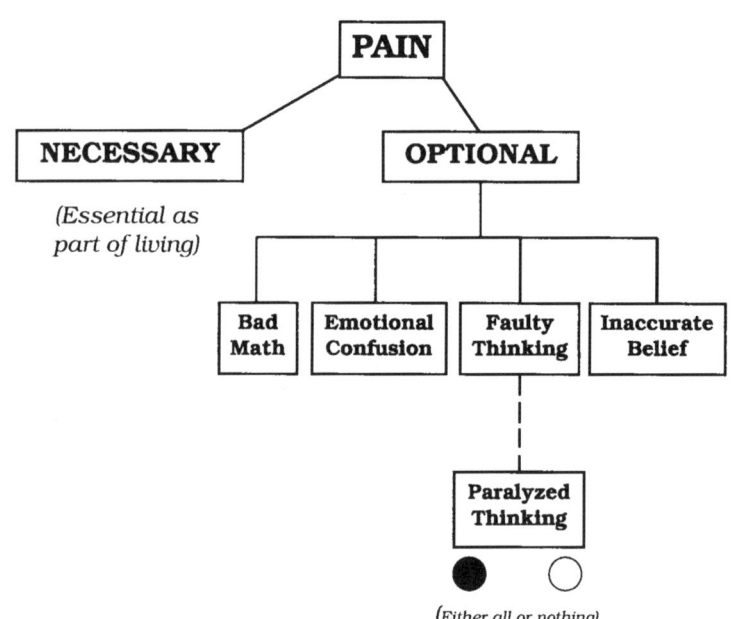

FIGURE 1-1

fering occurs when perceptions that are not helpful become our reality. When we perceive ourselves as unable or unwilling to lessen our suffering, we do not act to alleviate our discomfort. Finally, we come to accept optional suffering as necessary suffering, as our true experience.

Consider a more complex example of optional suffering in the statement, *I am unlovable.* There are four common cognitive (thinking) mistakes that contribute to making this unhelpful perception into a debilitating reality.

- **Faulty Thinking.** Faulty thinking is a rigid adherence to the "way things ought to be." Example: Life should be fair.
- **Emotional Confusion.** Elevating an emotion to the level of fact, and then acting on it, is known as emotional confusion. Example: I feel hopeless. I am hopeless. As a result, I act without hope.
- **Bad Math.** Bad math involves constructing an erroneous equation using always or never. Example: If I don't make this relationship work, I'll never make any relationship work. Bad math leads to incorrect conclusions.
- **Incorrect Belief.** Incorrect belief results from turning inaccurate thoughts or a set of assumptions into a full-blown belief. Example: My father doesn't love me. Therefore, I am unlovable.

There is a common thread between these cognitive mistakes. The fact is, these thinking styles can become habits that directly contribute to optional suffering. We all have made them to some extent. It is important to know the subtle differences between these thinking styles so we can recognize how each affects our perception. In my practice, I have found it useful to start with the Beck

Inventory, a series of questions that help clients identify and clarify their self-perceptions.

Our self-perceptions are shaped by our life experiences and by the way we make sense of those experiences, so I ask how the problem-solver sees the problem. Remember that our lives are always changing, and human beings react emotionally as well as physically to change. We must understand that if we feel pain as a reaction to change—whether our suffering is optional or necessary—it is real pain. It exists in the moment we feel it, and it has consequences for our future actions.

For example, while chopping jalapeno peppers for a Mexican dish I was preparing, I rubbed my eyes. The immediate acute pain burned an enduring lesson into my mind. I have not since repeated that mistake. I wish all of life's teachings were so swift and sure.

What we need to become skilled at is knowing our pain and interpreting its signals accurately. It is especially important to be able to discern necessary pain from optional suffering, because then we can select the appropriate remedies. Different remedies are needed for alleviating different types of pain, just as they are needed to remove different kinds of spots. Coffee stains, for instance, are different from grease stains. Different remedies are necessary, depending on the nature of the problem.

The dictionary defines pain as "punishment, penalty," and "distress of body or mind." By definition, what I felt the day I rubbed my itchy eye was bodily distress as a penalty for my lack of attention to the harmful effects of rubbing pepper juice into my eye. I wasn't thinking about what I was doing. My eye itched, I scratched it. I experienced pain as a consequence, which immediately got my attention.

Though this analysis is partially true, it's too narrow a view of that experience. The notion that pain is a punishment for wrongdoing is preferably avoided. With all the moments of pain we must experience in our lives, such a limited definition is not helpful. Yet in our culture, the idea persists that pain is punishment and that we are, therefore, always responsible for our pain.

## Pain as a Signal

I prefer an alternative definition: Pain is a signal indicating imbalance. Personal pain is an important, unique signal delivering valuable information about the source of the imbalance. Therefore, pain is not necessarily a bad feeling. It can become our ally in the process of change when we choose to understand it as personal biofeedback. Our responsibility is to pay attention to our own signals, to our own levels of pain. In this way, we become self-counselors able to diagnose and remedy the sources of our pain.

There are many ways we mishandle the information or misread the signals about the source of imbalance. Those will be discussed in detail in Chapter Three. For now, I want to expand the alternative definition of pain by introducing different ways to think about pain.

## The Problem of Pain

We need to think of ourselves as composite beings. We are mind/body/spirit entities. As composite beings, those three elements within us are as indivisible as a bubble. If we consider pain merely a body problem, we cannot properly correct the imbalance. If we assume our headaches are purely biological occurrences with no relation to our thoughts and feelings (mind and spirit), we will have difficulty lessening the pain. When I have a headache, I have my own headache—not an Excedrin headache.

To understand the interrelationship between mind, body, and spirit, we must first understand each. We probably know our bodies best of the three. Our bodies never lie. Physical discomfort is fairly easy to recognize. Many times physical injury has immediately visible effects. An ill-fitting shoe will quickly raise a blister.

Too much fun in the sun without sunscreen will cause a stinging burn. We can trust our biological feedback. We connect the cause with the effect. There are instruments to measure physical imbalances we can't see: thermometers, X-rays, blood tests, urinalyses, CAT scans. We also have a language to describe the experience of physical pain to others. Often we use metaphors such as "my throat's on fire," or "this flu's left me weak as a kitten."

We accept that body pain is knowable and that it is usually treatable. When pain is properly diagnosed, there are effective healing strategies to apply. Again, our language helps in the process of diagnosis. We easily respond to diagnostic questions: Where is the pain? When did the pain start? What makes it better? Worse? We also readily accept that body pain is often the result of either excess or deficiency, too much of one thing and not enough of another. We feel confident of our ability to correct the imbalance, even if that means simply giving our bodies the rest we need to heal.

My work as a therapist is specific to the sources of mind/spirit pain. Not surprisingly, nonphysical pain also signals imbalances resulting from excess or deficiency. Even though nonphysical pain often expresses itself in physical symptoms, mind and spirit pain are not as easily identified as body pain. Our language is not as precise in describing them. Clients find diagnostic questions about mind and spirit difficult to answer. That is why the Beck Inventory is so useful. The series of questions in the Beck Inventory identifies our perceptions about our relationships with self and others and our feelings of enjoyment, sadness, fear, and hope. Our answers to those questions allow us to describe and measure non-physical imbalances.

Once those perceptions are identified, we can search for the sources of and remedies for our nonphysical pain. In many cases, the pain is optional suffering. Its source can be traced to the four previously mentioned unhelpful thinking styles: faulty thinking, emotional confusion, bad math, and incorrect belief. Both separately and as a group these cognitive mistakes are examples of what I call paralyzed thinking, which is at the heart of all optional suffering.

## Paralyzed Thinking

Paralyzed thinking limits us to a choice between extreme courses of action—right or wrong, win or lose, all or nothing. Each of the four unhelpful thinking styles is distinguished by this choice-limiting perception. Paralyzed thinking is seductive because all things exist with their opposite. This phenomenon is explained by Sir Isaac Newton's Third Law of Motion, which states that each action has an equal and opposite reaction. Another example is computer logic, which is based on binary operations. The choices are only on or off. Because either-or thinking seems so logical, so familiar, and so right, we confuse it with being reasonable.

Paralyzed thinking simply doesn't work. It stunts our growth. We don't need much creativity to swing back and forth like a pendulum. When caught in this dualistic snag, we become uninspired. When we must choose between two unacceptable and unappealing options, mistakenly thinking that's all there is, we experience a dull hopelessness. I call this mind-cuffing. Mind-cuffing translates into mind/body/spirit imbalances as follows:
- Mind: Either way I lose.
- Body: My muscles ache and I have no energy.
- Spirit: I'm trapped, angry, stuck.

If you think only in opposites, there comes a time when you can no longer acknowledge the existing midrange options. Your spirit is stuck and your ability to act is frozen. People who cannot choose cannot act. Indecision becomes inaction over time. In reality, between white and black are all the colors of the rainbow. Forceful reds, vibrant greens, and inspiring brilliant yellows all lie between the absence of color and the combination of every hue.

When you have limited yourself to thinking in opposites, what you've done is taken reality and altered it. When black and white are the only options your brain is presenting to you, your perception is inaccurate. That perception doesn't match with reality. Tending to think too much in opposites means you are missing the multiple shades of color. Looking through either/or bifocals causes you to miss the hues.

## A Parable for Problem Solvers

Once upon a time, some people relaxing by a riverbank noticed a large number of dying trout floating downstream.

"Alas," the town mayor said, "these fish are very sick. We must cure them so we may be nourished."

The townsfolk pulled the ailing trout from the rushing stream. They took the gasping fish into their homes to nurse them back to health. Some trout managed to survive. But more and more dead and dying trout floated past the riverbank every day.

The situation grew critical. "What did we do to deserve this fate?" the townsfolk cried. "Who is to blame for this misery?" they moaned.

One day, a stranger from a village downstream came into the town.

"We are glad you have come," the mayor said. "We need all the help we can get to nurse our sick fish back to health."

"I cannot stay," the stranger said. "I'm on my way upstream to see what is plaguing the trout."

Problem solvers begin by gathering information. They ask questions. What is plaguing the trout? is a pertinent question, one that leads to an understanding of the problem. Problem solvers don't ask, Who is to blame for this misery? or What did we do to deserve this fate? Those questions don't lead to resolution.

In the parable, the stranger seeks to discover the root cause of the problem rather than merely the observable effects. The stranger who comes to the village acts like a scientist, prepared to examine what's behind the malady and experiment with a variety of solutions to the trout problem. Scientists think in terms of trial and error. They ask questions, beginning with *What's making this happen?* and *What if?* rather than *Why me?*

In CBT, we practice formulating and investigating helpful questions. My clients need to cultivate the art of effective questioning for two reasons: 1) to discover what lies beneath their thoughts, beliefs, and behaviors, and 2) in order to immediately rebalance what is out of balance. Effective questioning is a way to find the thinking behind feelings. It is also a way to direct energy toward short- and long-term solutions.

Early in the cycle of change, we must gather pertinent information about ourselves and our situations. The stress we experience in the cycle comes from both our inner and outer responses to change. Our primitive instinct perceives change as a threat, eliciting the fight-or-flight response. As we have evolved as thinking individuals, we can consider the additional options which lead to responses of acceptance and accommodation to resolve conflicts arising from lifestyle change.

Marie, Debbie, and Larry are all facing the reality of new lifestyles. They are forging new identities; redefining themselves. In therapy, they articulate and practice their choices and work through the consequences. What if Marie sells the family home and moves into a small apartment? What if Debbie decides to "come out" at work? What if Larry accepts a demotion in order to stay employed at his current job?

In my work as a therapist, I help clients build their problem-solving skills by utilizing the qualities of a resilient personality: connectedness, commitment, and self-control. Combined, problem-solving skills and the qualities of a resilient personality yield the ability to think clearly and function in ways consistent with what is in your best self-interest.

## Evidence of Clear Thinking

Characteristics of clear thinking include accuracy, flexibility, consistency, stability in relationships with others and self-image, and firm focus on personal goals. Clear thinking is possible when we move away from thinking in rigid categories or in terms of right and wrong, and open the possibilities of trial and error, of the shades of truth between black and white. I help paralyzed thinkers become rainbow thinkers, problem solvers who ask pertinent questions and experiment with a variety of possible answers.

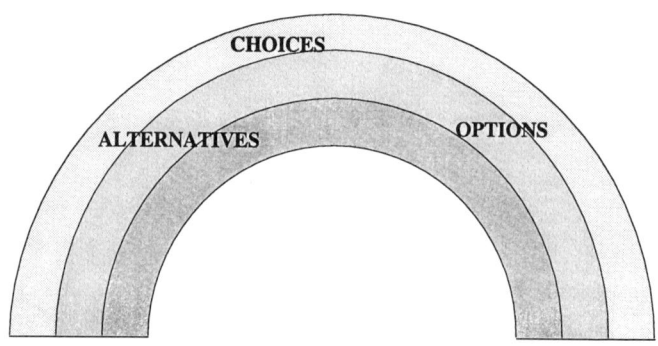

FIGURE 1-2

## Rainbow Thinking

Rainbow thinking is a training tool—it amounts to mind-stretching, to reaching beyond only two identified options. I use it to help paralyzed thinkers alter their thinking styles. Rainbow thinking creates and focuses attention on mid-range options, and sharpens an individual's perceptions for better accuracy. It unlocks the mind-cuffs, presenting a truer picture of reality. Naturally, there is still the matter of choice. Rainbow thinkers must still decide on their best course of action, and then act in their own best interest. Since paralyzed thinkers are mind-cuffed, training to become a rainbow thinker must include mental calisthenics.

Just as our bodies can perform certain exercises for better health and endurance, so can our minds. Just as an athlete may begin daily exercise with stretching certain muscles, a rainbow thinker may stretch the functions of her mind. An athlete's exercise program might include walking, running, swimming, stair climbing, or weight lifting. The program for rainbow thinkers includes option expansion, stretching belief, memory, reason, imagination, and judgment. It also includes practice in skill building.

### Getting Practical

The following exercise begins with an example of paralyzed thinking. As you work through it, you will use various cognitive functions to consider alternatives. Keep the following guidelines in mind as you prepare the worksheet:
1. Tell your truth. Focus on yourself—your experiences, your thoughts, and your feelings.
2. Be specific. Don't edit out what you think may not be appropriate.
3. Be open to new thoughts, feelings, patterns, and actions.
4. Recall other examples of change in your life.
5. Avoid self-condemnation.
6. Practice letting go of anger and fear.

### Exercise One: You Shape Up Or I'll Ship Out.

Choose a current relationship that you feel must change. The situation calls for negotiation between yourself and another person in your life. Consider what is problematic in the relationship. What does *you shape up* mean?

(Use a blank sheet of paper to complete numbers 1-5.)
1. State the problem in written form.
   Example: I don't get enough of your time.

2. Write as many problems as you can, and in the same specific way.
3. Consider your expectations of the other person and write them down.
   Example: I put my lover/friend/spouse/children first. I expect the same treatment in return.
4. Clarify those expectations and let go of those that have less importance.
   Example: My other friends are important to me.
5. List acceptable changes for each problem. State the changes as you would present them in a negotiation.
   Example: I would like us to spend one day per week alone together.
6. Imagine as many alternative changes for resolving the existing problems as possible, using the clarified expectations as you can. (Use a worksheet similar to the one in Figure 1-3 to list your ideas.)
7. On a separate page write these words: ALTERNATIVE thinking is necessary for change. Using the exercise, describe ways you now see in a different way.

| OPTION #1 | OPTION #2 |
|---|---|
| | |
| PARALYZED | THINKING |

**Results of Rainbow Thinking**

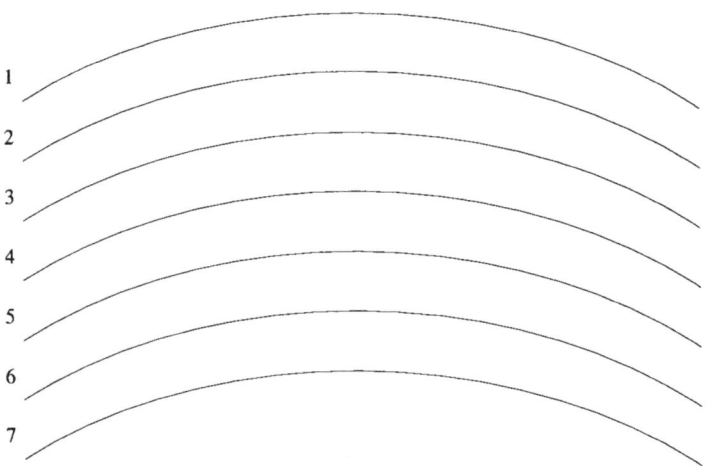

**Followed by Choosing**

**Here's what it's going to be:**
1
2
3
**Not:**
1
2
3

FIGURE 1-3

# 2

# HURTING

*H*urting is a theme throughout the cycle of change. Managing pain is an inescapable task. It goes with being human. Everybody suffers.

Pain is constantly in our lives. Whether we like it or not, hurting is here to stay. Burdens always turn up in one form or another. Gilda Radner said it well in the title of her book about dying of misdiagnosed cancer, It's Always Something.

*Marie was overwhelmed with grief. She felt acute shock and unspeakable pain, and was near despair. She had trouble getting up each day, avoided answering the telephone, and sat for hours idly staring, unable to cry. She was in a daze and uncertain about what to do next.*

*Some days Debbie felt sheer panic at her situation. Fear of what others would think, how she would explain her situation to her sons, and fear of rejection were overwhelming. The pain of keeping her conflict secret exhausted her. She questioned the cost of disrupting a ten-year marriage by pursuing this attraction to women.*

*Larry blamed the company for failing him. He stormed and raged at home, so angry he could not think clearly. He began drinking* to try to gain some control over his feelings. He was distracted by the emotional intensity of his feelings of betrayal and hurt, and totally uncertain what to do. He focused on repeating useless questions: How could this happen to me? This isn't fair. He began to withdraw from colleagues, feeling he could not trust anyone.

In Chapter One I distinguished between necessary pains of life and optional suffering. I want to say more about optional suffering and how this cognitive behavioral model is, as mentioned in the preceding chapter, something we can use to reduce the stress of change.

## Give Me Something I Can Use

I once ran ten miles with a man who had no feet. Pete Strudwick, an inspirational celebrity, was spearheading a March of Dimes run/walk in Dubuque, Iowa, a city of many hills along the Mississippi River. He had been born footless in Nazi Germany when Hitler was attempting to create the perfect race. In 1936, Pete's mother saved his live by smuggling him out of the country. When I met him, Pete was fifty years old and had run many tough marathons. He was using his disability and his accomplishments as a disabled athlete in his career as a professional speaker.

I was intrigued by how he walked, let alone how he ran. His lower calves sloped into what he called his "stumps," somewhat rounded solid bone. He wore custom-tailored red leather boots fitted as if on a horse's hooves. Tiny bells tinkled from his laces. He said they told him he was still kicking.

Walking was not as painful as running for Pete. "Imagine two tin cans strapped to your ankles, each step a jolt. That's what running feels like," he said. Midway along the ten-mile trek, as we approached a particularly steep Dubuque hill, everyone pouring sweat, some kids running in a bunch near us started grumbling about the route. "It's so hot! It's too hard! Why didn't they route the run on the flats? I don't like hills."

Without missing a step, Pete bellowed a response at the top of his voice. "Give me something I can use!" With that, he sprinted mightily to the summit. He had no tolerance for negative grumbling, facing that wall at West Third Street. At the moment he discarded what wasn't working for him, Pete drew on an inner source of power.

Pete chose to ignore the negative input and pass on optional suffering. He could have reacted to the kids' grumbling by saying, "Yeah, this shouldn't be this hard. Why don't those race planners get enlightened?" If he had, he would still have had the same hill to climb. But he also would have had to fight to recover the energy drained by such useless, negative thoughts.

Pete saw his task clearly—keep going, run the hill, finish the ten miles. He might have joined the complainers, but it would have been to no good purpose. He too was uncomfortable, yet he focused on what he could do right then in the face of reality. He continued doing what was possible. He rejected the option of engaging in a mental debate on the inadequacies of the planners. He focused his energy in a way he chose, which was to finish what he had planned to do.

## Cognitive Behavioral Training

Psychotherapy is a formal process of exploring pain to alleviate hurting. Cognitive Behavioral Training (CBT) is the hybrid model I use. CBT is a training method for changing misperceptions and behaviors.

There are many advantages to this model. The name, Cognitive Behavioral Training, indicates the essentials of the method:

- *Cognitive*
  The act or process of knowing or perceiving.
- *Behavior*
  1. The manner of behaving or acting;

2. The action or reaction under given circumstances.
- *Training*
  To form habits, thoughts or behavior by discipline and instruction.

One of the tools used in this CBT model for change involves accurate naming. The mind's job is to determine how to know what is hurting and how to talk about it. People often make some common mistakes around both of these tasks.

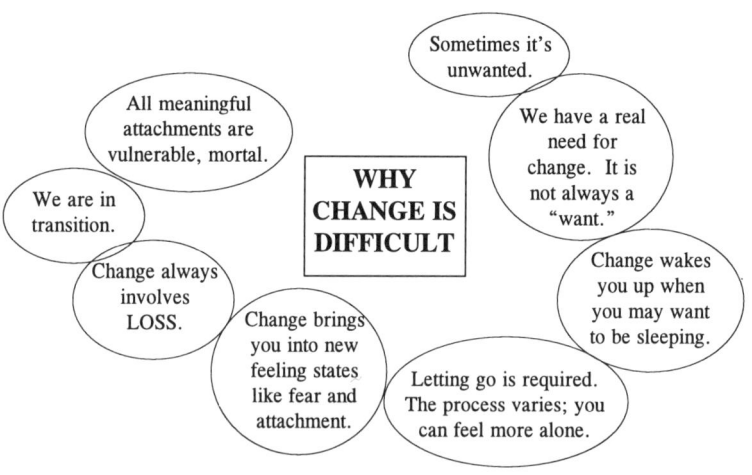

FIGURE 2-1

## Emotional Confusion

Emotions live in our bodies, and our bodies never lie. They tip us off when something isn't quite right, when we're out of balance. Emotional signals flash when we lose trust or feel coerced, manipulated, oppressed, lied to, or betrayed. Feelings are powerful sources of energy, and sometimes they get confused.

Consider this example of such confusion: Janet was a client of mine who experienced deep depression. Her emotional alarm went off in church; in fact, she reported spiraling into depression every Sunday. She felt lousy and fell into old familiar patterns of thinking and comparing. She thought, *"Since I feel so bad, there must be something terribly wrong with me."* Her next conclusion was, *"I have no future, but I have to live anyway."*

Janet didn't have much apparent love in her early life. There were periods devoid of affection all during her childhood. So she began incorrectly assessing herself as unlovable, and developed a self-evaluation tied to a lousy feeling. She still feels a deep, old soul sadness resulting from the absence of love. She feels frozen by expected grief for the life she dreams of but hasn't yet found.

Janet is actually experiencing a grieving spell. She is mourning the absence of love in her past. Having her present dream exposed in church, where she went to seek comfort, just confused her. Besides her negative self-talk, she feels both real and anticipated grief. Janet is mourning what was missing in her past and, in advance, what she longs to have in a family and fears she cannot have.

Naming the mush of feelings as an experience of loss is more accurate than labeling oneself hopelessly defective. Confusing sadness with anger is another common emotional mistake.

Accurately identifying feelings gives us important information. Anger is a powerful core feeling that connects us to our values. This emotion is often misunderstood because many of us learned that just feeling anger, let alone expressing it, is unacceptable. Since showing anger is wrong, we deny it and pretend not to feel it when we actually do. This denial leads to confusion, because we try to label the unacceptable anger with the name of another more acceptable emotion, such as sadness or guilt.

Emotions don't disappear when hidden away or given a more acceptable name like "sadness" or "guilt." We simply become more vulnerable and split away from our real response to provocation.

When emotions get too strong, there is an urge to do something—anything! When we yield to this urge we are taken over by feelings. This kind of emotional confusion can lead to dangerous, impulsive, self-defeating, self-injurious, risky, and illegal behaviors. It's as if the brain takes a back seat to the power of the hot feeling.

Anger is a signal worth listening to with special attention. The message anger usually conveys is: I'm being hurt, my rights are being violated, my needs are not being met. Anger may tell you that you are being asked to do more or give more than is comfortable for you to do. Anger tells you when something is not right. It may be telling us to pay attention to an important emotional issue in our lives.

Anger is a powerful force. We serve ourselves by learning to manage it for our own best interests. Practice worksheets in the Getting Practical section of this chapter will help you become more clear about yourself and your emotions.

## Elevating Feeling to Fact

Emotional confusion also describes the mistake of confusing feeling with fact. A statement such as *I feel hopeless, therefore I am hopeless* is an example of elevating feeling to fact. When we commit this error, we not only believe a feeling to be fact but also behave as if it were a fact. This is an inaccurate assessment based entirely on a feeling that we don't check out with our intelligent cognitive system. It is a signal that we are being carried away from logic and reason by a surge of emotional energy, and are ignoring the fact that thoughts influence feelings.

The "formula" associated with elevating feeling to fact looks like this (fill in the blanks with your emotional confusion):

*I feel* _____ *(emotion),*
*therefore I am*_____
*(emotion as fact).*

## Distinguishing Feeling from Thought

Another common mistake is not distinguishing between feeling and thought. This is the error of using feeling language with thinking content. Following are two examples:

- *I feel as if you don't like me.* (I feel… is feeling language; you don't like me is thought or opinion.)
- *I feel you're not listening to me.* (I feel… are feeling words; you're not listening to me is impression or interpretation.)

These are simplistic examples that reflect thinking errors that contribute to both personal and interpersonal stress. But this style of communicating can become troublesome, because feelings are elevated to the status of fact, and feelings are not the same as fact. I encourage clients who are trying to read their emotional pain with more clarity to stick with the basics: anger, sadness, happiness, fear, and guilt.

## Using Your Mind for a Change

The CBT model of change is about making the implicit explicit. It brings internal information out and into the light. We do this by stating feelings and emotions. In this way, we uncover truth and, of course, its consequences.

The goal is to raise awareness of our total picture by pulling out what is inside ourselves. We gather information through a kind of human biofeedback from our body/mind/spirit selves.

This model of change goes directly to what's hurting. The therapist pokes right into the place where it hurts, just like a doctor who investigates symptoms of pain by looking, listening, and touching. The purpose of discovering what's wrong, what's causing the pain, is to apply appropriate remedies to alleviate the hurting.

We do intentional thinking to make reasonable changes. This is where the mind comes into action. It is the mind's job to discern:

- What kind of pain is this?
- How is it remedied?
- What should be done with it?
- When is enough really enough?

We feel pain in all parts of our body/mind/spirit. There is no personal change without pain, and your attitude about hurting is important. As Figure 2-2 indicates, the self feeling the pain is also the self that must direct the healing. Often, if not always, a shift in attitude is the only way to make this healing possible.

## Advantages of Naming Your Experience

Mark Twain once said the difference between the right word and the almost right word is the difference between lightning and a lightning bug. Accurate language clarifies.

A complex interaction occurs between thinking, feeling, and behaving. Emotions move us, and we need to manage them. For example, when anger is moderate we can interpret it and usu-

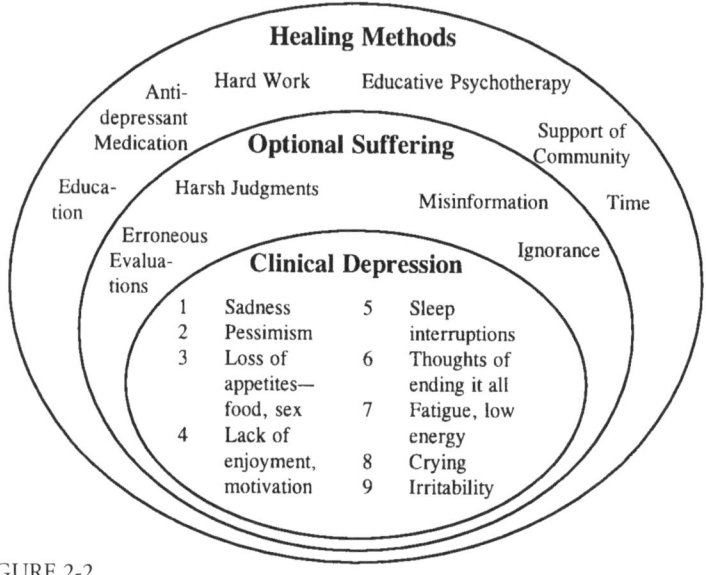

**Healing Methods**
Anti-depressant Medication, Hard Work, Educative Psychotherapy, Support of Community, Education, Time

**Optional Suffering**
Harsh Judgments, Misinformation, Erroneous Evaluations, Ignorance

**Clinical Depression**
1. Sadness
2. Pessimism
3. Loss of appetites—food, sex
4. Lack of enjoyment, motivation
5. Sleep interruptions
6. Thoughts of ending it all
7. Fatigue, low energy
8. Crying
9. Irritability

FIGURE 2-2

ally find what it reflects. Rage, however, is hotter and louder. Rage can be uncontrollable and very unproductive. The challenge is to balance ourselves as we manage our emotions.

You need your emotions just as you need your neck to connect your head to your body. We need our feelings to be human. Feelings best tell us how we are when they are moderate, not extreme. So it is in our best interest to understand how our emotions are triggered, maintained, and changed. This takes us back to what and how we think.

Naming is part of the change process. It helps connect you to yourself. Articulating feelings gives you tools for keeping clear with yourself. When you say, *"He made me feel…,"* another one of your warning flags waves as you catch yourself blaming someone outside yourself.

Naming is empowering. When you know what you're doing, you can continue doing it, stop doing it, or change how you do it. The key is to realize that when you can name something you're doing, it becomes something you can alter. You can also name other options, then choose from them.

Naming your perception requires referring to your internal processes of thinking and feeling. You are the one most familiar with your internal processes. Often, naming your perspective allows you to determine if you've sublet your thinking.

Perhaps you're stuck in some perspective you have internalized or believe to be true. When you articulate your conflict, you change your relationship to it. Naming your problem forces it, verbally and conceptually, to live outside your mind. This shows you your perspective in visualized thinking.

Matters of the spirit (love, inspiration, aspiration, hope, despair, discouragement, and so on) are more difficult to name. These feelings are part of change and, in my mind, part of soul. The more we can have some common language to describe the movements of the spirit, the more aware we are of this important com-

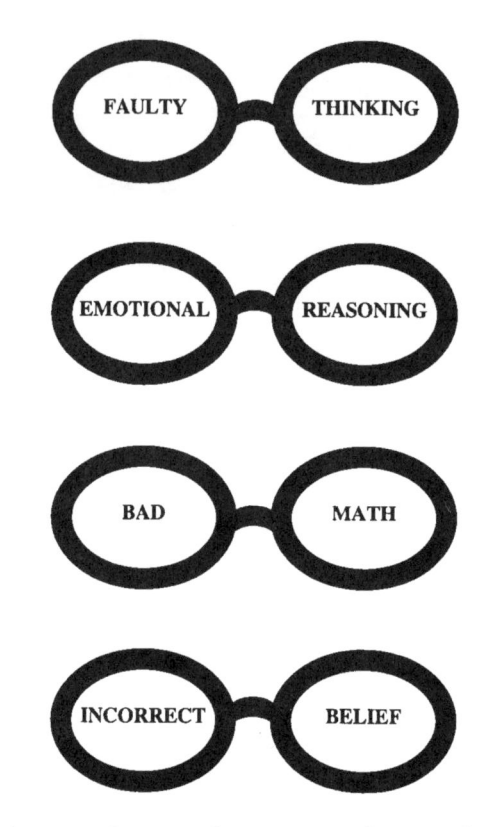

FIGURE 2-3

[FAULTY THINKING]

[EMOTIONAL REASONING]

[BAD MATH]

[INCORRECT BELIEF]

ponent. Unfortunately, spirit language is often confused with religious language. They are not the same.

Mind is not equivalent to brain, just as there is a difference between fact and metaphor. Mind, which is connected to spirit, is where symbolism lives. These matters are tricky to articulate, yet important nonetheless.

When we name something, we assign value to it. Naming what is troubling you helps you through the change process. When you name a trouble, you assign it some kind of reality. Most important, naming tells you how you define your struggle. It is the key to constructing a plan for changing something, and to determining if that construct itself is changeable. My definition of insanity is to continue to repeat what isn't working. This model of change is designed to stop insanity.

CBT is a proven, practical way to interrupt unhelpful personal habits of thinking, feeling, and acting. It is a model for reducing optional suffering. Unintended cruelty hides behind ignorance and ineffective habits. CBT offers training in breaking the cycles of unnecessary pain by interrupting the ineffective patterns that produce them.

Hurting can be quite distracting. As we can see from the lives of Marie, Debbie, and Larry, there are different kinds of pain. Obviously, it all hurts. How do you know what is hurting? Changes have a way of stirring up turbulence on different levels of our mind/body/spirit beings. We experience hurting on all these levels.

The following exchange with Janet is an example of the identification process:

*Janet:* *"I hate Sundays. I really have to fight with myself. I go to church, see all the families. Everybody's in little clusters. That's what I want and don't have. It's so easy for me to slip right into depression. I know my self-talk is bad."*

*CB:* *"What are you saying to yourself?"*

*Janet:* *"I have no future, but I have to live anyway."*

*CB:* *"What's not true about that? Find fault with it."*

*Janet:* *"Well, it's not true I have no future. I have a future. I just don't know what it is."*

*CB:* *"None of us do. We only have now, for sure."*

Janet was aware that this church experience repeatedly caused her to feel depressed. We continued mental flossing. Mental flossing gets at embedded material you might not know is there unless you look for it.

Janet had been to battle with this fear of the future many times. She knew going to church Sunday morning shouldn't cause a depression. However, it was a battle for Janet because of what she was thinking—her perceptions about being there.

When she took a mental step back from the situation, she recognized the progress she was making. Embedded in her *"I have no future but have to live anyway"* statement were various shorthand messages. These messages were more direct criticisms of herself. In the past, Janet sometimes became depressed so quickly that she did not know how it happened. The negative embedded beliefs were so familiar, she could zip through situations in emotional shorthand. Now her downward spiral still happens, but she detects it more quickly and weeds out the old beliefs.

Janet's self-talk included statements such as: *I'm unlovable, I'll always be alone, and I'll never be happy.* These mental snapshots, unexamined comparisons of herself to others, zoomed her to a place of misery.

Janet's depressive reaction was triggered at church when she observed presumably happy nuclear families: Mom, Dad, and the kids. She saw them as tangible reminders of her dream, which seemed to be slipping away with each passing year. Once this reaction rose to a language or image level, Janet knew immediately an old tape was playing. She had corrected it many times before.

**CB:** "What's some evidence that you have a life now?"
**Janet:** "I have friends."
**CB:** "Write their names. Make your evidence specific."
**Janet:** "I also have a job. And I'm writing a book about my experiences."

She listed her friends by name, and began feeling better as a more accurate picture came into focus. Reassessing involves carefully and thoroughly reviewing. In doing so, that which was previously excluded is included. More truth comes out.

Janet knew a lot about her habit of forgetting positive aspects of herself. I asked her to try a few sentence stems, which was a new process for her. She began with:

*If I let go of comparing myself to others, then*

_____.

Try it yourself—say the first five thoughts you have in response to this statement:

*When I let go of my self-critical judgments, then*

_____.

There is no better way to find out what's hurting than by writing some of the exercises designed to help you clarify what's causing your pain. The Getting Practical section that follows has several different guides to help you externalize internal reality.

After all, perception is your reality, but it may not be the true reality.

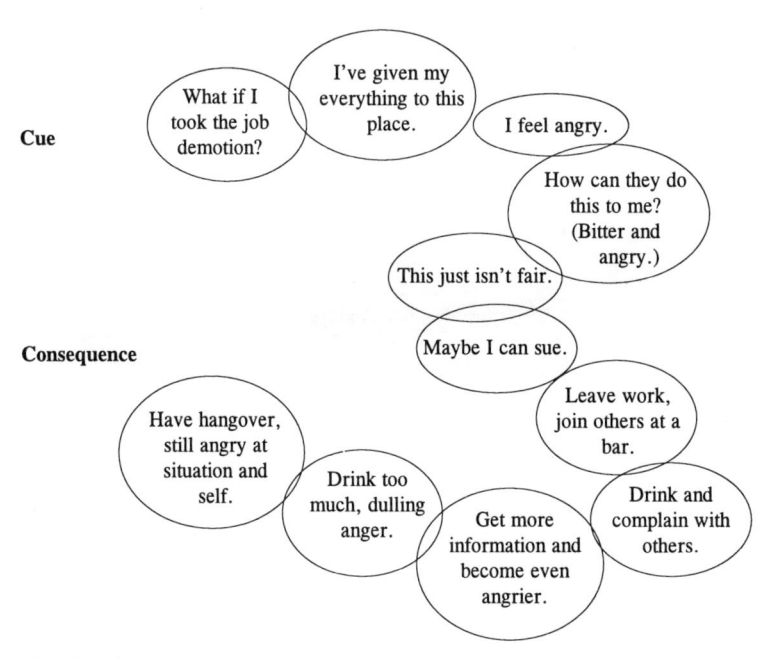

**Cue**

- What if I took the job demotion?
- I've given my everything to this place.
- I feel angry.
- How can they do this to me? (Bitter and angry.)
- This just isn't fair.

**Consequence**

- Maybe I can sue.
- Have hangover, still angry at situation and self.
- Drink too much, dulling anger.
- Get more information and become even angrier.
- Leave work, join others at a bar.
- Drink and complain with others.

FIGURE 2-4

## Getting Practical
### Exercise One: Behavioral Chain Reactions.

Larry prepared to work in a job he once supervised. He felt an immense anger toward the company. He remembered his glowing performance reviews, the hours of unpaid overtime, and his dedication to rising through the corporate hierarchy through hard work and loyalty. "I can't go backwards," he said. "It's too humiliating."

Figure 2-4 on the previous page is an example of how Larry's chain reactions might look if charted.

Using Figure 2-5 as a model, chart your own behavior chain reactions for a situation, event, or relationship that either needs to or has begun to change in some way affecting you.

### Exercise Two: Naming the Elements of Conflict.
1. State your problem.
2. State your perception of how you contribute to the problem.
3. State your perception of how other people contribute to the problem.

| 1<br>Activating event or stream of thoughts | 2<br>Body responses—feelings are felt in body (anger, fear, sadness, happiness)<br>Rate 1 to 100 | 3<br>Actions (withdraw, fight) |
|---|---|---|
| 4<br>Cognitions—automatic thoughts, embedded thoughts, images, pictures | 5<br>Distinguish accuracy of mind work: What is true? How true? | 6<br>Effects of rethinking<br>Rate 1 to 100 |

FIGURE 2-5

4. What are you willing to do to correct your part in the problem or conflict?
5. What do you wish your partner would do to correct the problem or conflict?
6. List two positive and two negative feelings you have toward your partner.
7. Write what for you is the present symbolic image of your relationship.
8. Describe the symbolic image you would like to have.

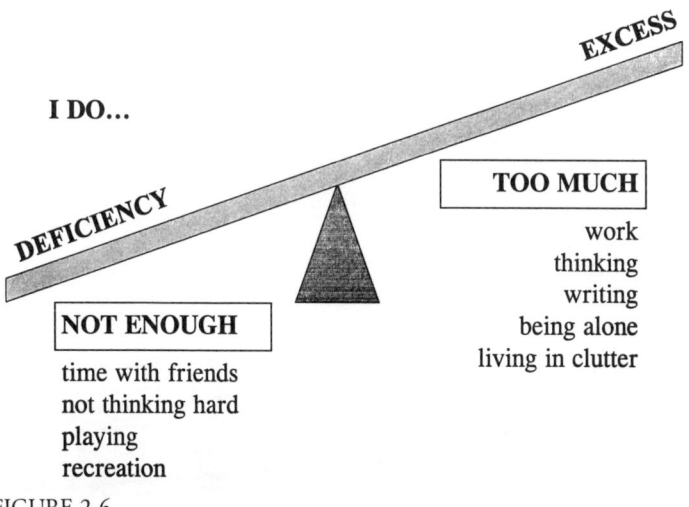

**I DO...**

**DEFICIENCY**

**EXCESS**

**TOO MUCH**
work
thinking
writing
being alone
living in clutter

**NOT ENOUGH**
time with friends
not thinking hard
playing
recreation

FIGURE 2-6

### Exercise Three: Naming Imbalances.

Using the example in Figure 2-6 as a guideline, list:
- Some things you don't have enough of
- Some things you have too much of
- Some things you don't do often enough
- Some things you do too often

# 3
# STRUGGLING

*Resistance is the common cold of change.*

My three clients shared another experience as they progressed through the change cycle. Marie struggled with the reality of living alone. Debbie knew that she loved another woman, but she struggled with the reality of living openly as a lesbian. Larry's position with the corporation would cease to exist, and he struggled with the reality of that change.

All three people resisted the changes they had to make. They struggled with their resistance to the unknown. Together, we must understand resistance—what it looks like and sounds like, what purpose it serves—to prepare for imminent change.

My dictionary defines "resistance" as *fighting against; withstanding the action or effect of; acting in opposition.* When faced with unwanted or painful change, or even difficult or unpleasant tasks, we fight and oppose their challenges. We endeavor to ride out the painful aspects and withstand the actions or effects of change. We use many strategies in our resistance; some are obvious and come from old learned ways of being, and some are more subtle.

One of my tactics is to avoid difficult tasks, or to resist change by shelving the problem. During the summer, while I was completing this manuscript, I sat down each morning to write. One morning the words weren't coming. I decided I needed a change of scenery. I thought that if I took my writing to the beautiful lake near my home, maybe I would feel inspired.

I set up my chair and spread my books and papers around me. The breeze was blowing, the birds were singing, and the sunbathers' radios were blasting. Swimmers were splashing in the water and the ice cream truck was ringing its bell. All these sounds and sights distracted me from the work I had promised myself I would complete. Why was I so easily distracted? Why couldn't I concentrate? Then I asked the question: Why was I avoiding my manuscript?

I heard the voice of my own resistance, the sound I call self-talk: *You've never done this before. Maybe you **can't**.*

Struggling with resistance involves wrestling with the internal and external knowns and unknowns of any given situation. My self-doubt led me to act in opposition to the task that lay before me. My resistance took the form of avoidance. I could find hundreds of distractions and "things that must be done" to occupy my time. After I had exhausted all of those, I could always reprioritize my other back-burner projects to further avoid writing. Finally, I could find myself inadequate.

In reality, I feared doing something I hadn't done before. My self-talk justified my fears. But my self-doubt only told a partial truth, that I had never done this before.

As I sat by the lake, I considered the other times in my life when I had tried something new and tasted the joy of a first achievement. Many things have changed in my life since I ran my first marathon, The Drake Marathon in Des Moines, Iowa, in 1977. Since then, I have learned of and maneuvered around many of my resistances. The T-shirt awarded to all marathon finishers, the one I couldn't wait to get my hands on, now serves as a dust rag. What is lasting and is more valuable to me than the coveted T-shirt is the sense of accomplishment I experienced from doing something I never thought I could do. My real keepsake from The Drake Marathon is my memory of changing my old habits, learning self-discipline, and persistently pursuing my goal by taking incremental steps. In 1977, I had been a nonathletic cream puff for sixteen adult years. I was a stressed-out smoker who never exercised and suffered from an asthmatic condition. Through the process of training for the marathon, my life changed. I am a healthier person now—that's indisputable. But more significantly, the experience changed my self-perception. I began to see myself in a different light. I am capable of seeking new challenges and meeting new demands.

To my self-talk at the lake, I needed to add a revelation from my experience. Yes, it was still true that I had not written a book before. However, I had run a distance of twenty-six miles without stopping. I had run that marathon step by step until I crossed the finish line. I could use my past accomplishment as encouragement now.

Using a positive previous experience (personal recycling, as I call it) is a valuable and informative tool for breaking through resistance. To proceed with change, we must become as acquainted with our successes as we are with our disappointments. We do this by noting what works, what doesn't, and what never has.

Remember, familiar things have a powerful pull for all of us. We are comfortable with certain thoughts, feelings, and actions. We are uncomfortable with uncommon things and new experiences. When we recall only our disappointments, we put off corrective actions and often worsen our current situation. We can drift into the it's-hell-but-it's-home pattern based on our feeling of security with the status quo. Even terrible discomfort can become comfortable over time. The way in which we perceive our current situation and our experiences can either add to our struggle or lessen our resistance to change.

## Acts of Resistance

The following are common *cognitive behavioral categories* of resistance for people struggling with change. These feelings are legitimate—although misdirected—uses of energy.

***Stewing.*** People who resist change by stewing about the future feel anxiety, even alarm, but cannot clearly state what is wrong. A client who is stewing might say, "I hate my job." In the same breath this client may also say with panic, "What if I lose my job? I have a mortgage. Oh, this will be awful!"

Stewing persons may notice physical stress symptoms such as frequent headaches, muscle tension, irritability, and sleeplessness. There is an element of catastrophe in their self-talk resulting from an imagined threat to their well-being. The stewing resistance keeps people from identifying the real problem. Instead, stewers focus on perceived or hypothetical threats and consequences. Their energy is diffused into ambiguous and overblown fear. They rehearse the imagined threatening situations in their minds.

Our ancestors lived with the present danger of being eaten by other predators. Their fear of being eaten by sabre-toothed tigers was reasonable. However, we now have more sophisticated threats to our personal security. Fears surrounding our acceptance by others and their approval can activate our fight-or-flight responses as surely as the growl of a hungry tiger. The response doesn't work, however, because the unnamed problem still exists. The conflict remains unresolved as we stew about what might happen and how we might feel when it does.

Debbie resisted the change in her life by stewing. *"I feel miserable,"* she said at the beginning of the process. Following that vague statement of imbalance, she started to stew. *"I'll be rejected. They'll think I'm a bad mother (or spouse, daughter, colleague,* and so on). *I'll be hopelessly scorned."*

The deeper issue for Debbie was camouflaged in her fears of what others would think. She couldn't get beyond this fear regarding her projected disapproval and rejection from others. Her sense of belonging was shaky, and her vulnerability to having other people's disapproval spur her into the stewing mode kept her focus on what she couldn't change. She could not act to resolve her misery as long as the problem remained vague and incomplete.

***Stuffing.*** People who resist change by stuffing their emotions carry on without acknowledging the pain they experience. Stuffers are initially aware of their emotions (anger, grief, fear, or guilt) expressed as pain. However, they believe that if they ignore the pain, it will go away. "I feel fine," a stuffer might say. "If I keep busy and don't think about it, nobody will know how bad I feel," is a more accurate and truthful statement. Often this inaccurate belief is a result of a lack of awareness.

Marie experienced intense rage when her husband and son died. For many reasons, both cultural and personal, she believed she lacked the ability to come to terms with anger and grief. By stuffing the anger she felt as a natural part of her grieving process instead of fighting through it, Marie's rage came out in unexpected ways. She could barely recognize the grief she had stuffed after her son's death, when it later reappeared as withdrawal and depression. Her grief peeped out as sarcasm and bitterness.

***Sentencing.*** People who resist change by sentencing are captive to one thought: "Who is to blame for what has happened?"

During the process of her resistance, Marie became consumed by self-judgment. She was a health-conscious person who read about and lived by preventive health care. (This was no small feat, considering that oat bran is the savior of heart health one day and a waste of time the next.) Marie had conscientiously cared for her son. She had sought the advice of numerous health professionals—dentists, internists, and ophthalmologists, among others—regarding his multiple maladies. He was living and working with undiagnosed Marfan's Syndrome, and shortly after his twenty-sixth birthday collapsed in his office. He died five days later following cardiovascular surgery. Marie was devastated. How could this have happened? What had she not done?

Resistance by sentencing demands that someone—either oneself or others—be judged guilty. This internalized blame targets an individual as the source of wrongdoing or omission. Left unexamined, sentencing can become habitual if the sentencer feels routinely responsible for every circumstance unsuccessfully concluded. Self-condemnation obscures a realistic picture of the problem, skewing and filtering out other pertinent factors.

Some sentencers focus more on convicting others. We are each ultimately responsible for our own behavior. Nevertheless, this truth doesn't serve the interests of one who is struggling with a tendency to become prosecutor, judge, and jury. The sentencer's self-talk takes the form of statements like, "My parents are to blame for why I'm so screwed up." Or, "This company is so crazy it's making me crazy to work here."

To break through sentencing as resistance to change, we need to use self-investigation to understand the underlying pain fully. While sentencing may be a necessary phase in clarifying the problem, there is not always one person or one thing to blame. Even more important, that one person is not always you.

***Shelving.*** People who resist change by shelving their problems are skilled in the techniques of avoidance. "I'll deal with it later," the shelver says.

Don't confuse shelving with a legitimate concern for proper timing. In the short run, it may seem reasonable to tackle a difficult change when you feel strong and certain that you have enough emotional resources in reserve.

If Debbie were to say, *"If I'm feeling this much pain just thinking about leaving my marriage, I'll never be able to go through with it,"* she would be resisting the change in her life by shelving. In my example at the lake, I found my inaction justified by a certain finality in my self-talk: *"Maybe you **can't**."* That didn't sound like simple procrastination to me. It sounded like resistance stemming from my inconsistent self-confidence. I was asking myself, Am I capable?

Women, especially mothers, have ample societal reinforcement for adopting other people's needs as their own priorities. When Debbie's issue seemed too complex and her resources for handling the change seemed inadequate, it's no wonder she spoke a shelver's words: *"The time isn't right now. I'll wait until the kids are older, when I have more money, when I feel stronger, safer, surer."* Debbie was excessively concerned with the needs of others as she undervalued her own.

Problems we shelve to avoid, just like emotions we stuff to ignore, keep very well over time. They don't dissolve or become less painful. Eventually, we must all face what we have stashed away.

**Storming.** People who resist change by storming misplace their emotional energy. Stormers commingle their pain with that of other people. The issues they must face become cloudy, unclear, and magnified out of true proportion.

One of my clients, Annette, suffered extended periods of depression for forty years. In therapy, she focused on her parents' unhappy marriage. She related to them as though they were divorced because the toxicity of their relationship was overwhelming. Her parents were not, and never had been, divorced.

Annette discovered she was feeling sadness over her parents' misery. There were many real losses she had experienced, losses that occurred because her parents' relationship was so unhappy. She needed to realize that she was experiencing not just her own sadness, but also her mother's and father's heartbreaks.

Annette's issues of intimacy and trust eclipsed the amalgamation of sadness, confusing her and leaving her drained and hopeless. Until Annette sorted through what pain was hers and what pain was theirs, her growth was stunted.

Storming can take other forms. Larry, for example, attached his anger about possible unemployment to that of his colleagues and saw it multiply.

Of all the forms of resistance, storming is the most external. We are all familiar with stormers who misplace anger. Having strung together sources of anger like beads on a string, they lash out at people both unsuspecting and undeserving of their rage. This behavior is commonly known as the kick-the-dog syndrome.

While it is true that provocation for anger is often external, we are still responsible for how we respond to changes in our professional and personal situations. The emotions associated with resistance by storming—anger, resentment, spite, revenge, sadness—are troubling. When experiencing these intense, accumulated, unexamined emotions, we can lose perspective. Our interpretation of the real situation can become distorted and skewed.

You may have recognized yourself somewhere in the above discussion. I don't want to leave you with the impression that these acts of resistance are wrong, or that you've committed a sin if you can say, "I do that." Rather, acts of resistance are natural, understandable processes of human development. These acts do, however inefficiently, produce information we can use. At their worst, stewing, stuffing, shelving, sentencing, and storming are ineffective uses of emotional energy. Recognizing the actions associated with resistance helps us realize we are on the wrong path, like taking our dry cleaning to McDonald's and asking for extra starch.

Resistance is an important rest stop as we move through the cycle of change. Thinking people who examine their lives share resistance as a common experience. All these acts indicate the need for change. When we notice the thinking process that produces our resistance, we come to a fork in the road. We then decide how to proceed in our own best interest. We must determine what we value enough to keep in our lives and what we can let go.

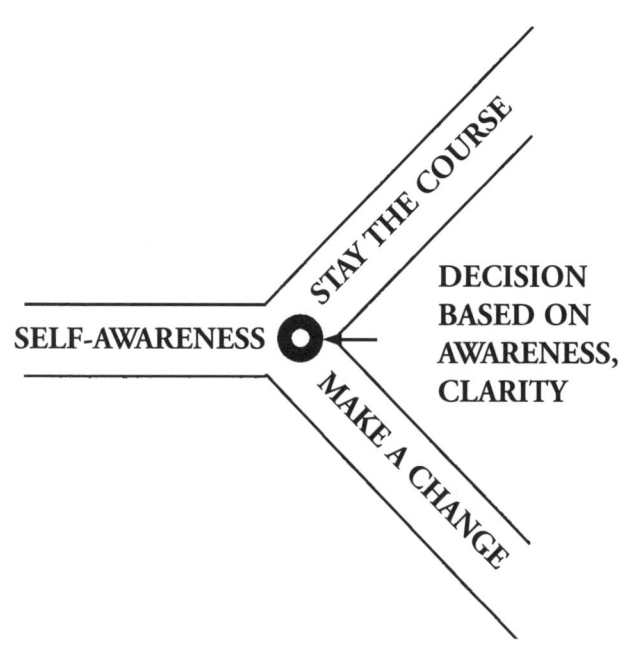

FIGURE 3-1

SELF-AWARENESS — STAY THE COURSE / MAKE A CHANGE → DECISION BASED ON AWARENESS, CLARITY

## Value Rigidity

"…The most striking example of value rigidity I can think of is the old South American Monkey Trap, which depends on value rigidity for its effectiveness. The trap consists of a hollowed-out coconut chained to a stake. The coconut has some rice inside which can be grabbed through a small hole. The hole is big enough so that the monkey's hand can go in, but too small for his fist with rice in it to come out. The monkey reaches in and is suddenly trapped—by nothing more than his own value rigidity. He can't re-value (sic) the rice. He cannot see that freedom without the rice is more valuable than to capture it."

—*Robert M. Pirsig, Zen and the Art of Motorcycle Maintenance*

Value rigidity is something we struggle with often in CBT. To some extent, we are all trapped by holding on too tightly or too long to the things we value. In excess, even our best intentions can sour. When we cling to anything or anyone beyond the point it is in our best interest to do so, we feel trapped. Like Pirsig's monkey, if we are to secure our freedom, we must reconsider the value of whatever lies in the trap we have designed.

Value is a relative concept based on our own individual belief systems. The old adage, one person's trash is another person's treasure, explains the individualized nature of value. It's easier to discern the underlying beliefs we use to attach value to external objects than to see how value rigidity functions in our internal, subjective thoughts.

Take, for example, the old-versus-new debate applied to objects rather than behaviors. Imagine that your dining room table is water spotted, scratched, and hopelessly warped. You decide you must replace it. Assume that all dining tables in the universe (brand new or antique) cost the exact same amount of money. For this example, money is no object. You have an unlimited amount so the new car battery or the dental exam aren't considerations.

You look at two tables. One is brand new, high tech, all lucite and lacquer. The other is rich old wood, older than your grandmother. You decide without much hesitation. You purchase the antique, a mirror-finished mahogany number with carved legs. You call your mother and invite her over to admire your acquisition.

"We had one just like this when I was growing up on the farm," she says. "I always hated that table."

If you had bought the high tech table, your mother might have said, "They sure don't make tables like they used to. There aren't craftsman like there were in my day." And you could respond, "This table is a work of modern art!"

Either way, we assign relative value to things both tangible and intangible based upon our own belief system. We are loathe to reject value once we have assigned it. Value can become an absolute, understood in terms of always and never. We become rigid in our thinking. Value rigidity as it applies to the change model induces us to make the cognitive mistake described as bad math in Chapter One. Once we begin thinking in terms of always and never, breaking through our natural resistance to new experiences and new thoughts becomes ever more difficult. At the root of this powerful resistance is not our experience, our perceptions, or even our thoughts. At the root of value rigidity is what we believe.

## The Roots of Resistance

Each of us lives as the sum of our individual genetics and the diverse and unique environments in which we were raised. We are products of both nature and nurture.

Genetically, we are a combination of our parents. Our cells were formed using information encoded in our parents' cells. Yet, that creation is entirely new and unique.

Environmentally, we are shaped by our experiences. Our emotional lives are formed by our interactions with those who love us and those who hurt us. During our early lives, when we are very impressionable, we learn to see and know the world. Informed by our impressions, we begin to construct our own realities.

Childhood is when we learn the rules by which we set our goals and determine our actions towards others. Rules are nothing more than consensual views of reality. Consensus helps people live together in better harmony. Rules not only serve as guidelines for our behaviors, but also provide a moral framework of codified belief around which we construct our own reality.

Take a common consensus rule, the Golden Rule, to illustrate how this works. This rule, Do unto others as you would have them do unto you, taught us as children to take turns on the slide and not throw sand in each others' hair. If we pulled another kid's hair, we were likely to have our hair pulled in return. Since we did not enjoy the sensation, we understood not to pull another's hair again unless we chose to suffer likewise. The lesson of the Golden Rule made good sense and was proven through childhood experience. It also has many necessary applications to our citizenship, and teaches us the skills of compassion and self-sacrifice. We can't always do what we want to do if we consider the feelings and needs of other people. We came to believe the Golden Rule was true and acted upon it in our lives. What could possibly be wrong with that?

Well, all things change over time, sometimes so slowly and so subtly that we don't see the change happening. The same compassion and self-sacrifice we valued as children can become resentment and self-denial if taken to an extreme. The skills that socialized us as children, made us credits to our families, and built our self-esteem can mutate. When the value of that belief is too rigid in the face of a changing life situation, we may lose self-esteem, become perfectionists, and demonstrate compulsive behavior.

When our concern for the feelings of others becomes neglect of our self-interest, we need to question the underlying belief. For some of my clients, the Golden Rule solidified into a belief that they must never put their own needs above the needs of other people. The original rule is a consensus rule and has value beyond our individual application. It serves a societal purpose. All rules protect what we value in life. However, the latter belief is a distorted rule and can definitely be changed.

I encourage creating or recreating self-rules by monitoring their effectiveness, examining their purpose, and updating them when necessary. Rules are not absolute. They are flexible and depend on context. When we break our self-rules, our thoughts and actions enter a state of flux. New options open to us. Changing self-rules involves alternative, or rainbow, thinking. Once we submit self-rules to a process of revaluation, every thought and action based on that belief also changes. Remember, we are mind/body/spirit beings and indivisible as a bubble.

Reconsider the monkey in the trap. Only his closed hand and the value he places on holding the rice stands between captivity and freedom. So reducing value rigidity is an intensely personal act. As Pirsig laments the fate of the monkey, he decides the monkey must slow down his process of reasoning. Stop and reflect. These are important steps the monkey must take to revalue the rice, seek his freedom, and change his fate. Holding rice in his monkey hand has always been a good thing and might well be again. However, his survival depends on his ability to let go of something he genuinely values, at least long enough to free himself from the trap.

## The Perfection Trap

Marie found herself caught in the perfection trap. Unable to let go of her belief that she was the perfect mother because she did everything right in caring for her son, she was unwilling to accept his death from Marfan's Syndrome.

Debbie placed the needs of others above her need to live an open and honest life as a lesbian. She could not let go of the illusion that made those she loved so comfortable.

Larry could not revalue his position at the corporation. So he obsessed that it was the only job he could ever do, and without work his life had no meaning. After all, he did everything right. Larry approached his work as a perfectionist does, considering all other facets of his life secondary. His job had his full attention. Now it was gone.

Perfectionism is the topic of many therapy groups I facilitate, and is an example of bad math. Robin, one of the group members I have worked with, explained her dogged pursuit of "perfect" motherhood. She determined her actions as a mother would be the direct opposite of her own mother's actions. She had learned through her own experience about parental deficits. She couldn't express any love for her mother and was, therefore, determined that her children love her always. Anything her mother did, Robin would never do. That was Robin's self-rule. The rule grew from her reaction to deprivation and neglectful parenting in her childhood. Robin compensated for her mother's lack of structure and parental involvement by setting stringent standards for her children to follow. Her standards were unreasonably high and impossible to maintain.

Everyone in group understood Robin's need to be loved by her children and her desire to avoid the errors her mother made as a parent. Robin intended to share a nurturing love with her family.

Another mother in the group testified that she had sworn off perfectionism. She described how stressful her rigidity had been for her family. She detailed the trade-off and accommodations necessary in an imperfect life. This is an example of one benefit of group therapy. Participants at different levels in the change cycle share new information.

Robin remained adamant that her perfectionism had value for her children. Her rigidity communicated consistency; her stringent standards for her children's behavior communicated her love for them and her concern for their well-being. But since Robin was a perfectionist, her way of doing things must, by definition, be perfect. Then what was the problem? Robin was sure that her children were miserable under her care. With this admission came an even more painful one, that she was "doing it all wrong."

The group comforted her by suggesting she was doing it right. She was just doing too much of it. *"I'm a terrible mother,"* she cried. *"I'm no good. I don't measure up."*

Instead of being a perfect mother, or even a pretty good mother, Robin perceived herself as a terrible mother. She concentrated all her energy on the pursuit of perfection in her parenting, but ended up opposite her goal.

Robin was still thinking like a perfectionist, in absolutes. There was only one goal worth pursuing. Perfection or condemnation were the only options. For Robin, there were no gray areas in her black-or-white thinking. Since her perfectionism failed to produce the intended results—the love of her children—both options caused her extreme pain. Her self-talk admonished her, You have to be perfect just to be okay. Instead of placing value on being a good mother, Robin valued only perfection. Her self-talk was filled with impossible expectations and condemnation.

## Thinking About Thinking

I suggested a CBT tool to help Robin reconsider the mental trap she had made for herself. This tool helps a person think about thinking. Whether we are aware of them or not, automatic thoughts (images, memory fragments, comparisons, assumptions, and judgments) constantly flash in our minds.

Thinking is silent talking. Silent assumptions are private and immediate thoughts. Thoughts become habitual patterns by which we compare ourselves to entrenched assumptions and recurrent judgments. Over time, thought patterns become so familiar that we fail to question their value or challenge their accuracy. Our thoughts ring true.

Before the group examined Robin's thinking in depth, we listened to her self-talk and considered the assumptions that lay beneath the words.

| Self-Talk | Assumption |
|---|---|
| *I'm a terrible mother.* | Since I'm imperfect, I'm a terrible mother. |
| *I'm no good.* | Since I'm a terrible mother, I'm a failure. |
| *I don't measure up.* | Since I'm a failure, my children can't accept me. |

## Mental Flossing

We uncover the negative assumptions imbedded in our self-talk statements by bringing them out into the open, usually through writing or diagramming responses to our self-talk. Once uncovered, the assumptions are subjected to one simple test for accuracy: so what if that's true? These exercises help the client with the process I call mental flossing.

Habitual or automatic thoughts are private, persuasive, specific, brief, recurrent, overblown, persistent, and imagistic. Mental flossing lifts automatic thoughts up into the conscious mind and out into the open, making them easier to see and to challenge. Left unexamined, automatic thoughts pervert our assessments of reality and skew our emotions.

## Getting Practical

Gathering new and clearer information is the goal of these exercises. Releasing the powerful hold that our unexamined assumptions have on our ability to make assessments requires that we revalue something we believe to be true about ourselves. It is a very personal activity. It is helpful to review your thinking style as it relates to your perception of any current situation, To lighten the load of this exercise, consider this story:

*A police officer pulls over a man who has been driving erratically for several blocks. One whiff of the driver's breath and the officer says, "You're drunk."*

*"Thank heavens," the man replies. "I thought my steering was going out."*

To accurately assess our life situation, we must assign relative importance and worth to those things under examination. Often we have already assigned value as part of our system of belief. Changing our assessments requires revaluing.

*Making Changes*

### Exercise One: The Feel of Resistance

Wear your wristwatch on the other wrist for twenty-four hours. Make a list of how many times you look for your wristwatch on the wrong wrist. Also note how many times you are aware of the difference and how you become aware (catching the watch on your desk or against a doorway, for example).

The following day, replace the wristwatch where you normally wear it. Are there any times when you look at the other wrist? If so, write them down.

### Exercise Two: The Mathematics of Change

We all have ambivalence about change. Part of us wants to change, but part of us tightens up, trying to keep everything just the way it is. That's because in order to make way for change, something has got to go, and we need to prepare for that.

Consider the following sentence:
*When I stop* _____,
*I'll start* _____.

Fill in the first blank with a behavior you'd like to change, and the second with a positive result. For instance: When I stop worrying that I'm not good enough at playing the trumpet, I'll start building the confidence I need to play better.

Below, list three behaviors or habits you would like to stop, and then write a corresponding positive result for each one. Be as specific as possible.

*When I stop:*
1._____.
2._____.
3._____.

*I'll start:*
1._____.
2._____.
3._____.

# 4
## CLARIFYING

*As hard as you think change will be, you usually end up wishing it had been that easy.*

As we continue to examine the cycle of change, we discover that Marie has spoken with a realtor. Together, they walked through the home she had made for her husband and children. Marie was overcome with grief. "I can't even think of moving," she told me on the telephone. "If I leave here, I have nothing."

Debbie, fully determined to "come out" at work, initially planned to make an announcement to all of her colleagues. Concerned that their collective reaction might be negative and that such a sensitive disclosure might become too quickly public and affect her husband and children, she became frightened. Her resolve crumbled. "I'm so selfish," she said. "I can't go through with this."

Larry, prepared to take the demotion, felt immense anger toward the company when he realized he would work at a job he had once supervised. As we've seen, he remembered his own glowing performance reviews, the hours of unpaid overtime, his dedication to scaling the corporate ladder through hard work and loyalty. "I can't go backwards," he said. "It's just too humiliating."

My three clients are grounded in the present and imagining the future. They have made their decisions and set their courses for action. The changes they contemplate have consequences. Each of them must now see those consequences clearly and determine how much grief, fear, and anger they can tolerate. They must see how the consequences compare to the pain they feel with the status quo.

## Mathematics of Change

In preceding chapters, we focused on thinking, especially the speed with which human beings process information in automatic thoughts. We looked at how thinking processes become paralyzed when we must act on incomplete information as an immediate reaction to changes in our internal and external environments.

As we move through the change model, we must clarify our perceptions and assessments so that we can act in our own best interests. So far, the discussion has been specific to immediate thoughts—that is, thoughts that occur as a response to a given stimulus and are specific to the primitive fight-or-flight reaction. Now let us turn to the topic of self-knowledge, which comes about from the process of reflecting.

Such clarification requires analysis—an investigation that will lead not necessarily to a lightning-fast decision, but to wisdom. I suggest that you read this material slowly. You're not scanning the newspaper for interesting fragments—the box scores, stock quotes, or your daily horoscope. The point is not to turn the last page of this book and say, "There now, that's finished." Attaining wisdom is a never-ending process. It is both a constant search and a continuing revelation. The wisdom you will gain is self-knowledge, sifted through your examined life experience.

You have already completed one Mathematics of Change exercise. Let's go back and understand the wisdom gained through this method of investigation.

Numbers are an important tool in analysis. I don't want to trigger your math anxiety with that statement. This isn't an algebra test, and you won't be graded on a curve. Numbers help us become organized. If you've ever made a list of tasks, you understand how assigning numbers to daily activities helps you set priorities.

Paralyzed thinkers struggle with concentration, memory, and focus. My clients and students have found that step-by-step formulas help them to clarify. Numbers document the thinking process and, as a result, illuminate emotional states and behaviors.

There are two types of numbers—cardinal and ordinal. Cardinal numbers describe the size of a collection of objects. Ordinal numbers refer to the position of one thing relative to another. For example, if I have fifteen pairs of shoes, I use the cardinal number 15 to describe the collection. If, on the other hand, I have three things to do before I go to work, I would use ordinal numbers—first, second, and third—to describe their relative position on my to-do list.

You may want to use ordinal numbers to rank emotions by intensity. My clients have found this method valuable; they like the neutral approach to personal change offered by mathematics. It avoids questions of causality and extracts the elements of blame and fault-finding. Bypassing the who-did-what-to-whom argument allows a more direct focus on what must change. You rank the intensity of your feelings on a scale of 1 to 10, with 10 being most intense and 1 the least intense. If you rank sadness a 10, your focus is not on the causes for sadness but on lowering the intensity of the emotion. What must change for the number to decrease? Change is seen as correcting imbalance.

The mathematics of change idea supports my no-fault approach to problem-solving issues of stress and depression.

Encouraging solution-focused stress management rather than dwelling on who to blame is a practical shortcut that saves precious emotional energy.

This change model allows us to view our problems objectively. Therefore, we can also accept the necessary changes objectively. We look for imbalances. What is there too much of? What is there not enough of? Instead of dredging up hurtful details that may have led to our situation, we see the big-picture view of the imbalance we experience.

The mathematics of change also happen on paper. Remember from your grade school experience the paper tablets and "No. 2" pencils with pink erasers? People who use math in their everyday lives also have erasers on their pencils. You made a mistake in addition, subtraction, multiplication, or division? Erase it! "Everybody uses calculators now," you say. Fine—the analogy works for calculators as well since they all have "clear" buttons. That's how clarifying works. The word means "to make clear." Check your work—that is, reexamine the thought process that may have led to an error in your solution.

## CBT Problem Solving

The therapeutic method of Cognitive Behavioral Therapy requires calm thinking and builds problem-solving skills. Client and therapist methodically correct the faulty thinking habits that inhibit the client's ability to function. Therapy occurs during twelve to sixteen office sessions and client homework. The client prepares written assignments designed to reinforce positive behaviors and enhance personal performance. Just like working through a math problem, writing forces us to organize our thoughts. It also does much more; writing uses two more senses, vision and touch, thereby involving other brain functions.

Seeing thoughts displayed on paper stimulates reflection that, in turn, opens the door to our inner lives. From there we can safely observe experiential knowledge, including our past mistakes. We are free to imagine future solutions. Reflection stirs our hope and builds our self-confidence. While inside our minds, our eraser is poised and our finger rests gracefully on the clear button. We become ready to engage in trial-and-error investigation and to see the process of change clearly to its conclusion.

The addition of new information makes us see things in a different way, but this also happens when we shift the emphasis of the information we already have. Reflection helps us do the latter of the two. A brief example: while we know that nobody can do everything, upon reflection we realize that everyone can do something.

The first step in CBT problem solving is to acknowledge the way things are. This is a process of cognition, our mind work that includes belief, memory, reason, logic, imagination, and judgment. We are also familiar with the cognitive mistakes that lead to paralyzed thinking. Let's review those now.

- *Faulty Thinking.* Faulty thinking is a rigid adherence to the "way things ought to be."
  Example: *Life should be fair.*
- *Emotional Confusion.* This kind of confusion consists of elevating an emotion to the level of fact, and then acting on it.
  Example: *I feel hopeless. I am hopeless. Believing this feeling to be fact, I act without hope.*
- *Bad Math.* Bad math is constructing an erroneous equation using "always" or "never" as the answer.
  Example: *If I don't make this relationship work, I'll never make any relationship work.* Other examples of this inaccurate way of thinking are: one = all, now = forever, and the past dictates the future.

- ***Incorrect Belief.*** An inaccurate belief is the result of turning an inaccurate thought or set of assumptions into a full-blown belief.
  Example: *My father doesn't love me. Therefore, I am unlovable.*

Since in CBT we commit our process of cognition to writing, we can catch ourselves in cognitive mistakes and actually see them in black and white. When we acknowledge the way things are, we try to express a mental picture of reality as accurately as we can. As you work through the exercises, be vigilant for instances of faulty thinking, emotional reasoning, bad math, and incorrect belief.

This process of acknowledgment does not require that you excavate great portions of your past. It is not necessary to collect much history that may or may not be helpful in explaining how things came to be the way they are. As far as CBT is concerned, acknowledged reality is specific primarily to the present. It is better used to answer questions such as *How can I manage my anger and sadness more effectively?* rather than *What events in my past are making me angry and sad?* Use your memory cognition only as much as it can help inform and describe present reality. I believe there is no virtue in repeating the same tragic tale seventy-five times. (There is, however, plenty of value in reassessing a tragic tale for the obvious purposes of avoiding past mistakes and encouraging healing.) The CBT problem-solving method focuses on primarily on today and tomorrow, not yesterday. It is a go-from-where-you-are approach. Throughout this program, you are encouraged to become aware of what is, become open to what could be, and become decisive about what will be.

Authentic change occurs from the inside out. It is deliberate, and emerges from the insight and resolve of the author/actor. Authentic change is not compliance or obedience to external mandates. With authentic change, there is an intentional shifting directed by the whole self—including mind, body, and spirit. It occurs when we release the deeper-felt vestiges of resistance. When we truly realize that something is actually going to change, change is guaranteed, because our part of the dynamic is going to change.

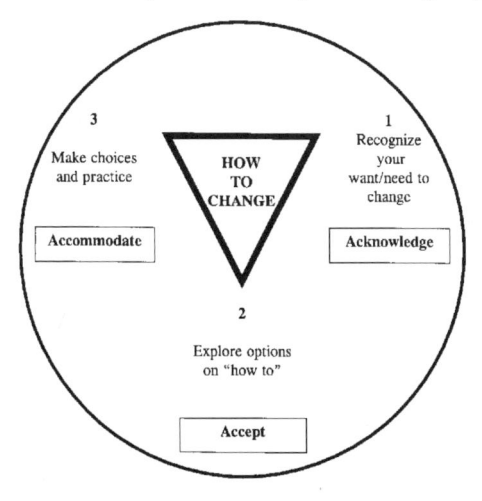

FIGURE 4-1

(This is precisely why it is so important to be clear about what it is possible to change, and what is not. Trying ever harder to influence what can't be changed is tantamount to hitting your head against a brick wall.)

## Evolutionary Change

Charles Darwin theorized that the natural environment selects survivors. Those biological beings best able to adapt to the ever-changing environment will prosper and multiply. According to this theory, an overpopulation of giraffes and other animals feasting on low-lying vegetation outstripped the food supply. Giraffes with long necks were able to reach the leaves still plentiful on higher tree branches, while short-necked giraffes starved. Nature selected long-necked giraffes as survivors. The genetic trait of long necks was then passed to offspring, while short-necked giraffes became extinct.

Thomas LeMark believed that, facing the calamity of mass starvation, giraffes stretched to reach higher and higher tree branches. LeMark then theorized that offspring can inherit acquired characteristics.

Sitting on the top of the food chain as we are, the giraffe's fascinating adaptation seems only a diverting curiosity. Darwin's theory survives; LeMark's has been debunked. The real lesson of the story of long-necked giraffes is how animals adapt to their demanding environments by nature and nurture. Adaptation is critical for survival.

Most of my clients come to me for help adapting to the stress in their lives. Stress results from our interactions with our environment, encounters with people, frustrations with situations, and discomfort with existential realities (death, guilt, fear, and so on). In the Getting Practical section at the end of this chapter, I've included a Litany of Common Stresses as a reminder that the stresses of life will remain with us on a daily basis. I encourage you to create your own litany.

Stress is a perceived threat to your physical, emotional, or spiritual well-being. It is anything that throws you off balance. The best way to adapt to multiple sources of stress in your environment is to clarify your perception of what is changeable, and use your mind for a change.

We humans have a resource the giraffes don't have. We have the ability to change our thinking. We can reason, change our strategy, negotiate a compromise, and even intentionally raise or lower our standards.

Some sources of stress are completely within our control. We have limited control over others. Unfortunately, there are some stressful circumstances over which we have no control at all. Obviously, different remedies apply to different situations.

In Getting Practical, you will analyze your litany of stresses according to the amount of control you have in each situation. You can change those things over which you have partial or complete control. Thinking differently is not always easy, but it is possible. Your perception of your situation as a threat to your well-being can significantly diminish, or at least become more manageable.

I encourage you to list those things you can change and those things you cannot. People who manage the stresses of modern life are flexible people capable of change. (And as we've discussed, change is just the way things are. It is here to stay.) The skills necessary for effective problem-solving regarding both chosen and unchosen change are acquired. LeMark was wrong—your children won't inherit this marvelous adaptation. They will have to learn it for themselves, as we do. And they can. Self-management is a learned set of skills that we can develop, revise, and practice over a lifetime. We can become proficient at managing the stresses in our lives. We can pass this precious set of skills to our children by example and by training.

This training, for our children and ourselves, often includes unlearning. Unlearning means ceasing a way of coping that is not working. In many cases it leads to changing your strategy.

## Getting Practical

The following exercises are designed to help clarify your present situation. Keep in mind that CBT is concerned with what is, what could be, and what will be. If you list a stress source that no longer exists in your life, one that you have dealt with and put away, make sure to identify it as one within your control. Recalling the past is useful as personal recycling, to remind us of our strength and competence.

It is noteworthy that the Chinese character for change is the combination of the symbols for danger and opportunity. Likewise, the logo for Cognitive Behavioral Therapy is based on a triangular symbol that also implies fear and chance. The CBT symbol acknowledges the possibility and difficulty inherent in the process of personal change. Authentic change requires motivation, inspiration, and perspiration as we work through difficulty and find our way to possibility.

## Exercise One: Litany of Common Stresses

Below are some common stresses of life. Think about each one that applies to you, and how much control you have over it.

1. Stress is paying higher bills on a lower budget.
2. Stress is not being able to communicate well.
3. Stress is suppressing strong emotions like anger, resentment, fear, and worry.
4. Stress is the death of a loved one.
5. Stress is being the victim of crime.
6. Stress is losing one's job.
7. Stress is having an automobile accident.
8. Stress is the unexplained cancellation of car insurance.
9. Stress is being audited by the IRS
10. Stress is an unfriendly boss.
11. Stress is parenting and/or family-ing.
12. Stress is not feeling well and not knowing why.
13. Stress is having your medication changed after purchasing the old medication at great expense.
14. Stress is the inability to find time to do chores, such as get your car into the shop, hunt for a new apartment, or look for a new house.
15. Stress is getting divorced.
16. Stress is losing track of time, whether it's waking up late or finding yourself celebrating another birthday without having realized the goals you had set for yourself.
17. Stress is making mistakes and feeling guilty, fearing failure.

## CLARIFYING THINKING WORKSHEET

| Blurred Thinking | Reasonable Counter-Statements |
|---|---|
| I have no control over what's happening to me. | I guess I have some control over what I do. But I still don't like either of the options. |
| "No control" implies 100%—all the control is outside myself. | I can stay in a downgraded position or be laid off. I do have the choice. |
|  |  |

FIGURE 4-3

Now make a personal list of common stresses and rank them in order of those you have the most control over. (The one you have the most control over should be ranked number one, and the one you have the least amount of control over should be last.)

## Exercise Two: Clarifying Thinking

Use the format in Figure 4-3 to list some examples of blurred thinking. In the right column, write at least one reasonable counter-statement for each example. A few sample statements are listed in the figure for reference.

## Exercise Three: The Ego Strengthening–Selfing Worksheet

This worksheet on the following page is designed to help you get clearer with yourself. The statements from that worksheet follow. Write your responses as indicated.

*I'm angry about*

_____
_____
_____ .


*When you*

_____
_____
_____ *(describe specific behavior),*
*I feel*_____
_____
_____ *(your feeling response).*

*What I want or need is*

_____
_____
_____ *(specific desired behavior).*

*I'm willing to*

_____
_____
_____ *(your part or limit).*

*I want*

_____
_____
_____ *(changed situation).*

# Accepting

# 5
## CLAIMING

*Only a revolution in mentality will change anything.*
—Malcom X

Marie felt angry at everyone, from the funeral director to the doctors who failed to diagnose her son's illness. She was uncharacteristically irritable and public with her anger. Beneath her rage was a growing awareness of the reality of her losses. She felt a mother's devastation over the loss of her child. Marie recognized her lack of power, her vulnerability, and her extreme aloneness. She was furious at the words "I know how you feel" from well-meaning family and friends, and found no term for a mother who has lost a child. A wife who has lost a husband is called a widow, and a child who has lost parents is called an orphan, but there was no name for Marie's new reality.

Debbie claimed her inner experience was valid. Acknowledging her feelings in the face of huge risk to her established lifestyle raised the possibility of pursuing them. She considered the consequences of a lifestyle change. Loss of prestige, status, extended family, societal sanctions, and dual income was only the beginning.

Larry had personalized his loss, realizing that his investment in the company was his identity. The intensity of his response forced him to realize he had been out of balance. He needed to prioritize his values to regain balance and to claim some of his considerable energies for his growth and health. He decided to diversify his energies and promised himself not to repeat the same mistakes: overfocusing on his career and neglecting his self and the pursuit of a fuller life.

Change involves loss; it means dropping and adding. While trying to stay with the status quo might seem comforting, avoidance of the agony of loss is only possible by not attaching to anyone or anything that can die or end. Loss is the most universal human experience there is, and loss and grief are absolutely unavoidable.

Through change we lose both tangible and intangible things. In all cases, we lose the familiar.

Consider trading in your old car for a new one. Your old one had its problems. The heater blew only tepid air, the driver's side window always stuck, and the trunk lock was broken. You had taken it to the shop many times for problems other than these. You had paid through the nose to have the brakes fixed and the transmission rebuilt.

The new car sits on the showroom floor with a red bow on its hood. It has that new car smell. You take it for a test drive on a cold winter day. The heater warms the interior within seconds. Just testing, you roll the window down and up again without the slightest catch. Back at the showroom, the salesperson pops the hood from inside the car. The hood release actually works!

You're annoyed when the used car manager gives you a low offer on your trade-in, and not just because you'd have to pay more than you had anticipated for the new car. Sure, your old car wasn't perfect. But it suited you fine. It got you where you wanted to go, started on the coldest days, and the radio always worked. In fact, you are quite attached to the old beater. You have feelings for it. It's a great machine.

You hesitate to sign on the bottom line. "I have to think about it," you say to the anxious salesperson.

"I'll see what I can do," the salesperson says. "Maybe we can give you a little more for your trade-in."

"I'll have to get back to you," you say though the half lowered window of your old car, and you speed away.

Actually, you're not as hesitant over the extra cash outlay as you are about suffering the loss of something familiar. These are common feelings all people have about making a change.

## Facts about Feelings

The common cognitive mistake related to feelings is emotional confusion. Most often it involves elevating an emotion (which is energy) to the level of fact. The individuals I work with in therapy are struggling with basic human emotions: anger, fear, guilt, sadness, and grief. Many people find it difficult to talk about emotions, and more difficult to manage them.

I remind my clients of the following:
- Feelings are not facts.
- Feelings are regulated by our limbic and autonomic nervous systems.
- Feelings are an important source of human energy, energy we can use for personal change.
- Feelings are not caused by events (situations involving people, places, or things).
- Feelings arise from how we perceive and assess events.
- Feelings in and of themselves are neutral—neither good nor bad.
- Feelings do not disappear when we leave them unacknowledged and resist them by stewing, stuffing, sen-

tencing, shelving, and storming. They remain and deepen.
- Feeling grief, fear, or anger about personal loss frequently manifests as depression. This becomes more complicated with unacknowledged loss and grief over unnamed, unknown realities.
- Managing feelings is a personal skill we can all learn through increased awareness, self-expression, and trial and error.
- Feelings must be acknowledged to be resolved.

Many of my clients need help distinguishing between feelings and thoughts. However, the following graphic shows that they interact, and that both influence behavior.

It is helpful to notice the interconnectedness of our mind/body/spirit. It is also important to understand the dangerous progression of unacknowledged emotions from powerful and positive energy to debilitating depression. I cannot repeat this enough: feelings of anger, fear, and grief do not disappear. They find some way to be expressed.

We have heard and seen many reports in the media lately about the consequences of repression, especially repressed memories. There is a debate raging within the psychiatric community

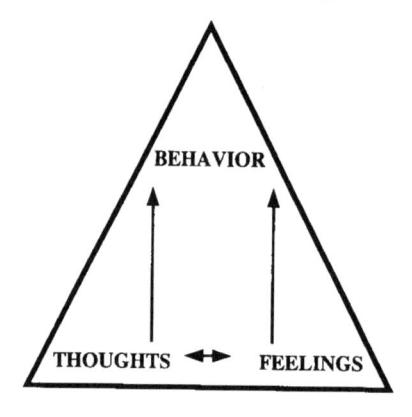

FIGURE 5-1

about the validity of repressed memory syndrome. Again, this change model focuses on what is, what can be, and what will be. We are not interested in dredging up the horrors of the past.

One of my colleagues who has worked with survivors of abusive relationships told me about a client named Alice, a woman in her forties suffering from depression. Alice only recently discovered that she was sexually abused as a child. In her case, unacknowledged anger had taken its toll. Alice had learned that anger was bad. Unable to express anger, she could not acknowledge it. My colleague worked with Alice to reassess her perception that anger was unacceptable. She taught Alice how to express the feelings she had stuffed deep inside herself for so long.

## Claiming Emotions

Both-and is the idea that combining opposites provides completion. It is the teaching of the yin and yang. In the last chapter we learned that to clarify our change process, we must acknowledge both the difficulties and possibilities inherent in the cycle of change. We must also claim both sets of consequences: loss and the appearance of something new.

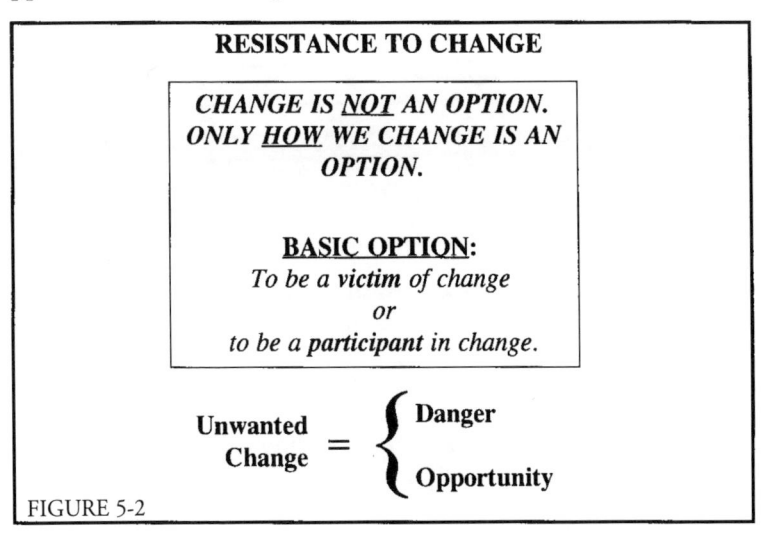

**RESISTANCE TO CHANGE**

**CHANGE IS NOT AN OPTION. ONLY HOW WE CHANGE IS AN OPTION.**

**BASIC OPTION:**
To be a *victim* of change
or
to be a *participant* in change.

Unwanted Change = { Danger, Opportunity }

FIGURE 5-2

For some reason, many people find it easier to claim the difficulty that exists in the changes they must make. Difficulty is familiar. It feels the same regardless of the situation. Change stirs anger, fear, grief, loss. Possibility, on the other hand, while unknown, stirs excitement and confusion. However, if we think change simply means exchanging fear for excitement, replacing loss with gain, we are thinking in a paralyzed way. Change means both-and, so conflicting emotions often co-exist at the same time. Reconciling seeming opposites by seeing them as both-and rather than one or the other is our constant challenge.

The outcome of change is not guaranteed, so there is a mix of feelings, including a temptation to stick to the hell we already know rather than risk the unknown. Most of us change when we feel the heat, not when we see the light, and we respond to pain when it gets severe enough or distracting enough. The readiness-to-change factor is quite personal to each of us. We are better prepared to undertake change when we realize that our choice is not between ambiguous either-or options, but rests in the completeness of both-and.

## The Power of Thought

You can feel the power of your mind as it changes. Intentional change requires that you make a choice. There is no more dynamic human process than choice—you feel it in your whole being.

Take my Uncle Bill, for example. He smoked two packs of cigarettes a day until he was hospitalized for heart problems. He quit that very day. He may have been thinking about quitting for a long time. His smoker's cough had become more pronounced, and his lungs felt tight when he walked downstairs to his workshop. Everybody he knew had given up smoking. Nobody wanted to sit with him in the smoking section at Denny's. Still, he claimed he enjoyed his habit. He feared he might be unable to quit.

Uncle Bill couldn't smoke in the hospital. No-smoking legislation had already banned smoking from patient rooms and guest lounges, even from the hospital grounds. During his ten-day stay, he could have set his mind on the fantasy of the first puff he would take the moment he was discharged.

He could have, but he didn't. Uncle Bill made an intentional decision to become a nonsmoker. He felt the power of his mind calm the physical pull of his fifty-year addiction.

## Readiness

When we are ready to change, we choose to change. Our decision comes from inside ourselves. This is a different process from mere compliance with an external law or rule. We feel the power of our mind, our willpower, and our courage. Our fears and excitement stir, and our personal resolve and self-confidence increase as we meet the challenge of change, step by incremental step.

A person needs confidence to change. The process of claiming implies that we "own" what is real in our experience and freely discard whatever we're clinging to that prevents us from moving on through the cycle of change to the realm of new possibilities. The ancient Chinese symbolized change as both danger and opportunity; this is still true today.

Claiming is an inner shift in self-realization. We accept necessary suffering (actual difficulty) and jettison optional suffering (perceived or misperceived blocks) to gain possibility. We step into the unknown, aware of the danger and confident in our ability to manage what lies ahead.

Think of a trapeze artist releasing one bar while reaching for another. She is confident that the distant trapeze will fall into her grasp. Does she know this for sure? No. While she hangs freely in space for a moment, she is aware that she has never been in this exact space in time before. It is new territory. But she is also aware of her successful experience, her careful training, and personal skill. (Perhaps most importantly, she knows that she is the one to make the change!) When she feels the bar connect with her outstretched hand, she is ready to move on to the next, more distant trapeze. She is trusting herself here and now as well as drawing on past experience and knowledge of herself in order to move on. *"I am doing this"* becomes *"I can do this."*

I'm not suggesting leaping unprepared into whatever comes along. I advocate reasonable change. The model described in this book teaches a method of planned personal change.

However, we cannot always schedule change. A lot of life seems to be made up of shifting to plan B, and this is a source of some of the stress of change; unwanted, untimely, and surprising changes can throw us off balance. The accumulation of too much change too fast interferes with our ability to plan and respond well.

My personal account in Chapter Six documents events from 1991, after my father had been misdiagnosed. This true story includes examples of key concepts of the cycle of change, such as optional suffering and the mathematics of change. Obviously, it is a story close to my heart. I used the cycle of change as my map for moving through the unwanted experiences of my father's illness and death.

## Getting Practical

The work involved in claiming who you are delves into the past more than any other change cycle activity. You must consider what you know, and how you came to know it. You must also name the mistakes you have made.

As with all CBT exercises, the underlying guide with those that follow is to use the past only as much as it informs the present and illuminates the future. The focus of claiming is to accept what is true about yourself and reject what is either outright false or a misperception.

| DANGER | OPPORTUNITY |
|---|---|
| Loss of the familiar<br>•<br>Loss of competence and self-esteem<br>•<br>Loss of traditional views of power and direct control<br>•<br>Loss of status and prestige<br>•<br>Loss of friends<br>•<br>Loss of job security<br>•<br>Loss of understanding of the culture<br>•<br>Loss of predictability<br>• | Opportunity to move into a more desirable position (inside or outside the company)<br>•<br>Opportunity to learn new skills and develop expertise<br>•<br>Opportunity to expand network<br>•<br>Chance to advance due to understanding of and preparation for change<br>•<br>Opportunity for personal growth through risk-taking (develop confidence and self-esteem)<br>•<br>Opportunity to try something different or always wanted to do |

FIGURE 5-3

It is important that your thinking about yourself be as precise as possible. The exercises are designed for you to document information about yourself. Remember, even mistakes increase self-knowledge. Difficulty and possibility coexist to complete one another.

### Exercise One: Mistakes I Have Made

Set a timer for ten minutes. Write your recollection of a past mistake, what you learned from it, and how you learned the lesson.

### Exercise Two: Dismantling an Unhelpful Belief

Read the list of unhelpful beliefs presented in Figure 5-4. Refer to them as you complete the exercise following the figure.

| CONTROL | BELONGING |
|---|---|
| 1. I'm just the way I am. I can't change. <br> 2. I am a victim of circum-stances. I am powerless. <br> 3. If I worry enough, this problem should get better or go away. <br> 4. I can't cope with difficult or scary situations. <br> 5. There isn't enough time to do what I want. | 1. I must please others. <br> 2. I can't stand being separate from others. <br> 3. I get love by earning love. <br> 4. I can't rely on others for help. <br> 5. It's too risky to trust others. |
| **ACCEPTANCE** | **COMPETENCE** |
| 1. I have to achieve to be OK with myself. <br> 2. There is something fundamentally wrong with me. <br> 3. My feelings and needs aren't as important as others'. <br> 4. I should _____. <br> 5. I can give but I can't take. | 1. I should be perfect (in all things). <br> 2. If I take risks, I'll fail. <br> 3. Success is everything. <br> 4. If I stop worrying, something bad will happen. <br> 5. I can't make mistakes. |

FIGURE 5-4

This exercise is a straightforward, cognitive defensive against unhelpful thinking, self talk, or beliefs. Write your responses to the following:

1. Recognize your belief as unhelpful. State it.
2. Find fault with your belief. Document evidence. This is not true because…
3. Stop basing your thoughts and actions on this belief. Document actions you intend to stop.
4. Restructure a more helpful, more accurate belief. State it.
5. Begin basing your thoughts and actions on the new belief. Keep notes about the results.

6. Expect resistance to changing this belief. List some behaviors you can recognize as resistance.
7. Reinforce the accuracy of the new belief, in spite of resistance. Document second-effort moves.
8. Continue behaving and thinking in light of the new, more reasonable belief—even though it may feel phony or awkward. When you persist, the new belief will become real and feel more natural with practice. Keep a written record of changes you notice as you continue work on this step.

# 6
# RELEASING

*Proof of the spirit: Laughter, forgiveness, music, awe,
love, dance, mercy, self-sacrifice, death.*

Folk singer Arlo Guthrie once said that if you were to learn today that you have a terminal disease and decide to live your life differently, there is something wrong with the way you're living your life now. Arlo apparently had reason to think about this subject. His father, Woody, died of ALS, known more commonly as Lou Gehrig's disease.

Living with the reality of death raises the awareness of life. On April 23, 1991, both my father and I began living our lives differently, and we both began to learn a great deal about the process of releasing. Dad had suffered eighteen months with what his physician had diagnosed as an esophageal hernia. On that April day, he and I heard these life-changing words from the head surgeon at the Mayo Clinic in Rochester, Minnesota: "You have inoperable cancer."

Disbelieving, I asked to see proof. On both the current X-rays and those taken eighteen months earlier, the surgeon traced the metastases from the original site in Dad's esophagus into his stomach and lungs. The physician's voice rose with irritation that such an obvious malignancy had been missed. Further, the misdiagnosis had gone unchallenged for all the months since the first X-rays were taken.

I have several years of experience in the health care profession as a therapist. In all those years, I have never heard such candor from a doctor when describing imminent death. "What made you wait so long to seek another opinion? You've been so stoic. I can do nothing for you now," the surgeon snapped at my father.

I knew why he had postponed getting a second opinion—Dad had thought he had a hernia. He had taken his physician's advice regarding treatment: He took only small bites of food, chewed thoroughly, and avoided anything too spicy. And he just went on about the business of living his life as he always had. In December and January of 1993 he visited the six of his eight children who live in California. Then tax time lured Dad back to Iowa; he managed his former CPA firm during the tax season. Some of those old clients still preferred Dad's special touch and called him from semiretirement year after year.

When his symptoms had seemed to be getting worse despite his precautions, Dad had intended to seek a second opinion, and I had intended to accompany him. It just never seemed very urgent. Only when I heard Dad answer the specific questions the surgeon asked about the progression of his malignancy did I realize how much pain and suffering he had kept to himself. I don't know if anyone had any idea how much suffering he had endured for all those months—I didn't.

After the consultation, I pulled the doctor aside and asked for an estimate of the time Dad had remaining. I had a sense that his time was very short, but I did not want the doctor to make the pronouncement to my father directly. As a chaplain, I had counseled many family members of terminally ill patients, and I had always objected to physicians who told patients how much time they estimated was left when they rendered a terminal prognosis. I knew too many patients who accepted such educated guesses as fact and then ignored the variables of healing. These were patients who resigned themselves to the statistics and closed themselves off from the possibility of change. It is very difficult to counsel those who rely on authorities other than themselves.

This doctor, who had shown so little hesitation expressing his opinions earlier, refused to offer one now. Instead, he said, "In the brief time I've seen your father today, I've heard a lot about your family. I understand that the eight children are living all over the country. You all come and be with him now. He's a good man."

It was the easiest decision I ever had to make. I took a leave of absence from my work as a therapist at Riverside Medical Center.

## How Much Pain Is Enough?

Dad had never been ill, and he was not a complainer. Beyond describing the infrequent common cold, he didn't know the language of sickness.

The surgeon had very aptly called my father "stoic." For one who has never been sick, the process of chemotherapy can be unimaginably frightening. The suffering is magnified for one who is unable to express the fear and pain.

After my first visit to the oncology clinic with my father, his inability to talk about himself surprised me. When asked how he felt, he would say only "fair," "not too bad," or, almost comically, "could be better." He offered no clue about his experience of pain or his acceptance of the process of treatment.

I saw my father seven days a week, but he didn't share his thoughts or feelings very much. I remember coaching him to give me details about the course of treatment—I wanted to know more about what was happening with him. He responded directly to my questions, but offered nothing more.

Dad tried valiantly to get into his office each day. He had business to finish. Some days, after insisting that he needed to be at the office, he was too weak to leave the van. His secretary and other colleagues came out to the parking lot to greet him on these occasions.

Several weeks into treatment he was hurting all over. He was weak, gasping for breath, coughing, and vomiting. I could tell he was also worried, fearful, and hoping against hope. Finally, after all my insistence that he speak up for himself, he reported to the oncology nurse that he had been coughing excessively since the treatment began. I could hear the irritation and fear in his voice.

"That's the way of it," the nurse replied.

"How can I fight this thing when I can't even eat?" Dad asked. "I keep losing weight."

"It can be that way," the nurse said as she turned her back and started to walk away.

I hated her for saying that. She had looked my father square in the face and said, "That's the way of it. It can be that way." The conversation was closed as far as she was concerned.

After a few seconds of stunned silence, I said, "What about THC tablets? I've heard that patients experience appetite stimulation and pain relief from marijuana because of the THC that's in it."

"We don't do that here," she said, and continued out the door.

I felt so angry as I stood there with my dismal array of options dismissed as figments of my imagination. I recalled when I left my work with acutely ill people, after eight years of counseling the sickest of the sick, because I had come to view the world as too dark. I had become too serious; there wasn't enough balance, enough exposure to the light.

After his oncology appointment, Dad was too sick to stop by his office. His suffering was visible, and his spirit was sinking. No one could predict how long he had before the malignancy would kill him, but no one ever expected the chemotherapy to do any more than buy time. I knew he would suffer; I just didn't know how much.

Then, things took a turn for the better when my sisters arrived from California. They showed less patience with Dad's condition than he and I had, and their perspective turned out to be helpful; we all took him to the hospital emergency room with a firm "something-has-got-to-be-done" attitude. The real change happened when Dad met Catherine, the admitting nurse for the cancer unit.

I had heard my father interact with all the health professionals involved in his cancer treatment up to that time. It seemed as if he had refused to talk about his pain or describe what hurt. Watching him with Catherine, however, I realized it wasn't that he was unwilling to disclose his level of pain and his feelings about his terminal condition—he was reticent because he didn't have the skills to talk about what was happening to him. He simply didn't know how.

Catherine made it very clear that his message of pain must reach those who could help. "I see here that you're a CPA," she said. "Let's put some numbers on this pain. On a scale of zero to ten, with zero being no pain at all and ten being the worst pain you've ever had, give a number to the pain you have right now."

With the help of this nurse, Dad learned to communicate about his pain. He learned to pin down his pain by intensity, location, and frequency. Catherine gave him lessons about how to cough to minimize his discomfort. She taught him how his pain medication worked and how to piggyback medications. He learned to use the meds to the best advantage by taking them at key times in the pain cycle. Dad was an eager learner, and grateful for the help. Soon he had less discomfort and less fear, and was experiencing slightly more control with an out-of-control situation. Effective pain management reduces optional suffering, and good communication finally made this happen.

He became active in his treatment, and had a say in how the medical staff would treat him and his pain. Giving Dad the tools to break through his communication problem was absolutely essential to those positive developments. Since he was dealing with a progressed metastasis, there would be no cure. However, with comfort measures, his spirits improved, as did his ability to cope with his condition.

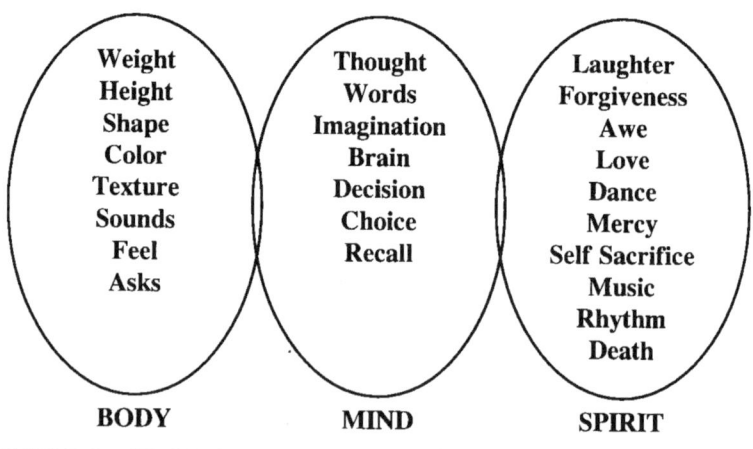

| BODY | MIND | SPIRIT |
|---|---|---|
| Weight | Thought | Laughter |
| Height | Words | Forgiveness |
| Shape | Imagination | Awe |
| Color | Brain | Love |
| Texture | Decision | Dance |
| Sounds | Choice | Mercy |
| Feel | Recall | Self Sacrifice |
| Asks | | Music |
| | | Rhythm |
| | | Death |

FIGURE 6-1. "PROOFS OF HUMAN BEING"

## Proof of the Spirit

The moment of death is proof of the spirit.

Dad slumped to the floor while I was walking him back from the bathroom. I made him as comfortable as possible and held him there. He was lying in the living room—the same place he had watched his eight children wrestle each other, play Scrabble and Monopoly, and sing and dance. There were thirty-four years of memories there.

As the minutes slowly passed, I heard his breathing change. I turned to his nurse and said, "He's dying. Please get my mother."

My mind flitted back to the moment, weeks earlier, when Dad had asked me to sign the "no resuscitation" order on his Living Will. "Dad, are you sure about this?" I had asked. He nodded, and we both sat on his bed and wept.

There was always much left unspoken between us. He was difficult to talk with about personal things. We avoided politics, because we never could agree. Like many fathers and daughters, we talked about sports, his business, people in the news, the family. We told each other jokes.

Many years ago, I worked my way up to telling him I loved him. Oh, I had written it thousands of times in our frequent correspondence over the years. But I had never said those words while looking into his eyes. I had witnessed so much death in my work and had seen so many people burdened by unspoken truth; I determined to tell my father in my own voice that I loved him, and to keep my regret list as short as possible.

I stroked his head and named each of his eight children, in birth order (that was the way he always kept track of us). I said, "Mary Beth loves you, Dad, I love you, Tom loves you, Kevin loves you..." and so on, telling how each of us felt about him.

I saw the lines of tension, fear, and pain fade from his face. He was dying. The weight of his hand in mine changed; it felt heavier somehow. The word *countenance* came to mind as his facial expression became more youthful. "Let go, Dad," I said. "Be at peace."

His lips looked fuller and his eyes appeared to soften. He was the same young man who sat for his high school graduation picture. He was letting go without any further resistance or struggle. Through flowing tears, I said my last good-bye to my father.

"What does a vignette about her father dying have to do with this book about change?" you may be asking yourself. When my father died, two and a half years into the writing of this book, I decided to share some of what I learned about releasing from the experience of my father's death.

The death of a loved one is one of the most drastic forms of change. It is both an act and a process. I bore witness to my father's last breath, to his releasing from life. With this act of release, neither of us could be the same as we were before.

For the person who loses someone close, grieving spells are part of the process of releasing. Just as we cannot always schedule change, neither can we schedule the grieving spells that are part of the process that supports the decision and act of releasing.

The process of releasing means living with and through the loss on an ongoing basis, and this involves necessary grieving spells along the way. My spells included releasing blame for human errors that occurred in my father's diagnosis.

Mourning is the immediate phase of grieving. Crying, aching, wandering in a daze, even seeing him walk through the door as he always did and hearing his voice, were parts of my mourning. I sensed his presence in his clothes and other belongings, and ten days after his death I had to stop myself in the act of picking up the phone to give him a call.

Grieving is part of releasing, but releasing is something we do again and again as we grieve. This is because grieving is soul work, and does not follow a schedule; the reorganizing of your self around the absence of the other is not a linear process.

I used the cycle of change, the model for planned change that this book describes, as a guide for adjusting to the unwanted change I've just described. The ingredients of change are the same for both wanted and unwanted change, and it is useful to have a roadmap for both kinds, because both mean going places we have never been before. If we stick with this map for change, we gain familiarity with the ingredients, and this builds trust in ourselves as we journey through the cycle.

## Grieving Losses

Grieving what has been lost is the work of the body and the mind as well as the spirit. We must not assume that working through grief has one set of instructions, or that the path that will lead us out of the grieving process is obvious or easy.

As interested as people are in the possibilities of life after death, for the survivors it is the life after loss that is most relevant to the discussion of change. In the aftermath of Dad's death, I decided to use the remainder of my leave of absence to grieve. I set out to complete my process in the time left to me before returning to work. I have since given a name to my experience—microwave grieving.

My father taught me the value of maps. They are necessary when going places one has never been before. They show you different routes, and help you stay on course. When I made a map for my path through the grieving process, I first needed to make a key of instructions that set the parameters of distance, direction, and destination. My key looked like this:

1. **Feel the pain.**
2. **Write about the feeling.**
3. **Talk to others about the loss.**
4. **Decide in what spirit to live because of the relationship.**
5. **Take comfort in all the life that remains.**

Even though I drew my map to mourn my father's death, I came to see that every change in our lives—no matter how small—is a death of sorts. If you leave a job or move from your home, you experience a little death. When you end a relationship with someone, or lose your innocence and see the fear and disappointment in the world, you must grieve a little death. The stress of change comes from the loss of the familiar.

Grief is an expression of the value of what once was. It is a mind/body/spirit response that translates: "This was important to

*Releasing* 91

## THE CYCLE OF CHANGE

```
        12
     RECYCLING
  11              1
SELFING       QUESTIONING
 10                2
PRACTICING       HURTING
  9                3
CHOOSING       STRUGGLING
  8                4
PLANNING       CLARIFYING
  7                5
REDIRECTING    CLAIMING
        6
     RELEASING
```

FIGURE 6-2

me." That understanding illuminated the cycle of change for me. In a real sense, we are valuing and revaluing as we do these activities. The twelve chapters in this book describe this process.

In a previous chapter, I discussed how faulty thinking can allow a good rule for human interaction to become an unhelpful, even debilitating belief. I used the Golden Rule as an example of a necessary lesson (compassion for others) that can become an unhelpful belief that the needs of others must always take precedence over the needs of self.

Think about when you were a child. Just about the worst thing anyone could call you was selfish. If you found value in your gifts or achievements, then people probably accused you of conceit as well.

You are no longer a child. You cannot accommodate the consequences of change unless you define yourself. You must think for yourself as well as of yourself. That means valuing your achievements and honoring your personal, unique gifts.

Remember the example I used of the South American monkey trap? Once we learn to value things in the world, we must also prepare to revalue them in the face of change. Always use as your guide the words that express your understanding of the value of what you have lost, the words used to let go: This was important to me. Honor those words as your own true definition of self. Say them as you release what you no longer possess.

## Releasing Means Letting Go

Change has become the norm for our way of life, personally and professionally. Many of us need to reevaluate the way we relate to change. We should accept change as the norm, not a cause for alarm.

Still, resistance remains a natural reaction. It's part of the grief process. Some resistance shows itself in our clinging too tightly or insisting we change that which is not changeable. This resistance takes a great deal of energy and does not really resolve any problems one is having with change.

Most people experience a turning point when they release or let go of resistance and begin dealing with reality. Times of frustration may follow that point, yet you are not as immobilized as before.

Letting go has more to do with focusing on what is now than:

- What was
- What might be
- What ought to be
- What you wish would be

Letting go is practicing the art of detachment. A person of great wealth can be attached to her wealth. Another can have nothing and be attached to having nothing.

Here are some other characteristics of letting go:
- Letting go is admitting our inability to control some things. For example, we cannot make someone love us.
- Letting go is acknowledging that some situations and outcomes are not in our hands.
- Letting go is an act of will—a decision, if you will.
- Letting go is also a process, marked by gradual changes leading toward a particular result.
- Letting go means not adjusting everything to my desires.

## Getting Practical
## Exercise: The Art and Science of Letting Go

The following are some letting go methods that have worked for individuals going through changes:

1. As we sort through our ambivalence about change, we can uncover what we are clinging to. Think as clearly as you can of what it is you are letting go. Articulate this to yourself; write it down. It will serve as reinforcement for both your decision and your process. For example, I am letting go of blaming myself for being disorganized.
2. If you usually like challenges, find the challenge for you in the new situation. It may be learning new and difficult material, working with new people, or not giving in to negative thinking. Accept the personal challenge of the change and concentrate on that.
3. Pay attention to today, to here, to now. Live in the present. Wishing for yesterday when things were easier, or waiting for tomorrow when things will be better, prevents you from committing yourself to the task at hand.

4. Refuse to be a victim of change. Take positive action in those parts of your life where you have control—your attitude, your friendships, your creativity, your mind, your physical health.
5. Reality is a great convincer. Find out the facts rather than spin your wheels on possibilities, rumors, lack of information, or wishful thinking.
6. Do not be surprised when you have feelings of sadness, anger, longing or grief along the way. We experience feelings with losses and limitations. This does not invalidate our decision to let go. Acknowledge feelings, feel them, and let them be a legitimate part of the process of letting go.
7. Prepare for the worst-case scenario if you sense a change about to happen. For instance, be prepared for a layoff or a breakup. Review the options and rehearse your optimal response.
8. Talk with friends about your feelings. Find out that you are not alone in your frustrations and discover what other people have done to let go of their resistance and frustrations.
9. Trust the process is another perspective that will help you focus on those things for which you have responsibility. You trust that the process will continue without your direct supervision.
10. Find a meaningful phrase like "microwave grieving" or "bad math" to use as a reminder that you waste a great deal of energy trying to control things that are beyond your sphere of influence. Pay attention to those things that you can affect, and let other people take care of the rest.
11. Visualize yourself letting go of your resistance. Deliberately create a mental movie, complete with

sound effects and feelings, of letting go of your irritations or breaking through a barrier. Imagine that you are breaking through a wall, or that all your negativity is in a box and that you are finally dropping that box off a high bridge. Be aware of the heaviness of the box and how you feel when you let go of it.
12. Change is not an option. Only the way you deal with change is an option. Take time to select and read new articles and books on change. Letting go is essential to change. Objectivity puts change into a broad perspective so we can see patterns.
13. Each of us has our own style of letting go. Familiarize yourself with your method of letting go. Get to know your pattern.

# 7
# REDIRECTING

*Life can only be understood backwards, but it must
be lived forwards.*
—Soren Kirkegaard

It took more than six months for Marie to accept that her life had irrevocably changed. She accepted that she would have to start looking at her future differently. She began to read material about grief and joined a grief support group. The group members gave her a sense of being connected to something and enabled her to talk about Mark's death. They helped with concerns such as disposing of the men's clothing filling the house. She began to pay more attention to her house, consciously redirecting energy to her intimate space and imagining a difference. Practical concerns began to intrude. She wondered with whom she would process her decisions.

Debbie impulsively left her family and began living alone. She began redirecting her energy into identifying the details of what she wanted. She allowed herself to be more complex, being aware of feeling sadness and relief at the same time. She allowed herself grieving spells. She assured herself, "No matter what happens, I can live alone and be all right." She began seeking friends who supported her lifestyle change.

When Larry stopped denying that he had losses to grieve, he was able to let go of his dream of retiring at the top of his company ladder. Forced change compelled him to ask himself not only, "What do I do now?" but "What do I want to do now?" He became able to redirect the energy he had used for blaming into questioning what he would like his future to include. He called his employee assistance resource person for referrals to career change seminars, and made an appointment with his physician to check out his headaches and fatigue.

We have two hearts, one for being and one for meaning. The first is a physical heart, a muscle that has size, shape, texture, and temperature. It circulates and exchanges blood rich with oxygen for blood depleted of it. We understand the value of the physical heart and realize that it is prone to illness. Physicians now educate us in the value of lifestyle changes—diet, exercise, stress management—as well as medications that can prevent diseases of the heart. These prescriptions represent behavioral and biochemical changes that can promote lifelong wellness. If we choose to make those changes, we accept the idea that change occurs for our own best interest as a result of our commitment to our personal well-being.

Chapters Five through Eight are specific to activities of acceptance. The focus of those activities—claiming, releasing, redirecting, and planning—is accepting the reality of change. True acceptance involves a shift in yourself—internally and externally.

The second heart is the metaphysical heart with which we feel love and hope, fear and despair. So as we redirect our energy and reform our behaviors in the face of change, the second heart is vital to the process. We consciously decide to claim the realities of change and release the past, and then we realize the experience of having new energy.

Before we act, we need to carefully consider the consequences of available choices. Redirecting energy requires that we explore options in order to clearly see our alternatives. Now is the time for glimpsing something different from what has been.

Letting go of unhelpful perceptions allows us to access the emotional and spiritual energy we once used to keep ourselves stuck in the status quo. Accepting that alternatives do exist creates momentum for change. Rather than feel this energy dissipate in anxiety over possible outcomes, expend it to power your imagination.

Most of my clinical experience has been with individuals experiencing stress and depression. I have seen the tremendous loss of vitality, self-worth, and pleasure that profound depression causes. During treatment, there may be moments when the realization of past loss produces anxiety. Some clients blame themselves for their depression. They insist that depression is their fault. Others deny having any control over their depression. They feel overcome by everything. These people may be sleep deprived, unmotivated, or unable to perform even the most automatic and mundane daily tasks. Those who have never experienced the lethargy of depression may find it difficult to comprehend being unable to brush their teeth, or sleeping through the night in the same clothes they wore to work during the day. Depression is a debilitating malady, one that robs a person of the felt sense of himself or herself. My clients desperately want to feel better, but are unable to recall how they felt before the onset of their depression.

## ALTERNATIVE THINKING

Neither blame nor denial is helpful. Blaming yourself for your depression only stirs up shame. Shame has a powerful paralyzing effect. Saying you can't do anything about it negates self-control and increases helplessness. Both statements sap the energy necessary to fight the downward pull of depressive symptoms.

Since this chapter is about redirecting energy for making positive change, let's remember first that the process of change requires flexibility and imagination. Alternative thinking frees the imagination. The second important point to remember is that solutions will not occur when the abstract goal is unappealing or impossible. Therefore, making a change in your own best interest requires both a flexible thinking style and a realistic appraisal of possible alternatives. (One of the most effective problem-solving tools I know is to make lists of options; there will be more on this in Chapter Nine.)

In my work with clients, I marvel at how even a slight shift in perception changes the way things are. Time and again while facilitating group therapy I witness the singular and collective powers of the mind once there is the will to change. Clients begin to reinterpret past experiences, imagine new possibilities, and create new realities. This is evident in three vital and dramatic perceptual shifts:

1. Aspiration awakens.
2. Heroes surface in the telling of their own tales. They stand as a witness of one.
3. A person's courage and daring rally to meet the challenge of change.

The word courage is derived from the Latin root *cor*, meaning heart. Courage dwells in what I've described as the second heart, the source of human spirit. (Our second heart, the intangible one, is not so easy to discuss. Matters of the human spirit often get mixed up with religious contexts.) The spirit I'm referring to contains our impulse to connect. Courage gives us the mental and moral strength to resist opposition and implies firm resolve in the face of difficulties. It is a quality of temperament that enables us to hold our own against adversity and resistance, including interference from others.

Reforming a mindset includes willing something different.

Both courage and will come into the picture here. Will is the power of the mind to choose and follow through in that direction, and willing means wanting to change and being responsible for what we are redirecting ourselves to. It also means determining how we spend our time from now on. A will to change is a quite personal thing, as it connects to our desire. At this point of redirecting we reroute our energy; we do without what was and forge ahead towards what will be.

Will and courage redirect our energies. Courage allows us to accept that we cannot change the past, and yet can reflect on how the past continues to contribute important elements to the present.

Hindsight is a legitimate perspective. Reorganizing the nature of a situation or event after its occurrence informs our insight. Insight, penetrating mental vision and understanding, is what ultimately influences our foresight and allows us to see with our hearts. Only when we see with our hearts do we get down to the business of change.

Once you say the words of truth to yourself, there is no stuffing the genie back into the bottle. Self-knowledge brings with

FIGURE 7-1—ONCE YOU SAY THE WORDS OF TRUTH TO YOURSELF, THERE IS NO STUFFING THE GENIE BACK INTO THE BOTTLE.

it certain personal responsibilities. We are responsible for doing the best we can with what we have, given our personal insights and the emotional support available to us from others.

## Changing Your Worry Program

As I've said before, much of my work with clients involves examining mindsets. Clients contribute the content, while I contribute the form. We work together to identify and dismantle unhelpful mental habits, some of which have grown from frequent thoughts into full-blown beliefs.

Now that audiotape technology is becoming obsolete, I describe the mind as a kind of compact disc. You can hear the same song with very little sound distortion every time you play the disc. When Ella Fitzgerald sings Cole Porter songs on my CD player, her voice sounds the same no matter how many times I listen to it. If I want a different tune, I change the cut.

Cognitive Behavioral Therapy is useful for changing our programming. When we identify mindsets as no longer helpful, it is in our best interest to modify, restructure, or replace them. This is possible even when the mindset has been in place for a very long time. Since CBT involves both thought and action, it is very effective in controlling irrational behaviors.

Lessening persistent worry is a good example of employing a rational strategy to combat an irrational behavior. The example is also as close to universal as any example I know. Everybody worries. I used to worry more than I do now. I tend to be a reflective person by nature, so I ponder not only my life but also the lives of others. Psychotherapists are trained to observe and investigate human experience. The profession causes much vicarious anxiety. In 1992, I tired of hearing my own anxious thoughts. I made a resolution to reduce my worry. I determined to "practice what I preach."

Each of us has our personal worry program, self-designed to torment us with disturbing thoughts and keep our fears poised for immediate replay. This is not to say there isn't a lot happening in our troubled world to provoke anxious concern. After considering the fate of a planet beset by war, hunger, crime, and environmental destruction, there is an array of personal worries to disturb our inner tranquillity. Some common sources of anxiety include:

- Relationships
- Children
- Career and Money
- Health and Aging
- Community

It is interesting that these sources of anxiety are also sources of great fulfillment, self-esteem, and joy. Interpersonal relationships, children, careers, physical and emotional wellness, service to the community, and even the process of growing older are sources from which human beings derive a sense of purpose, freedom, and achievement. This is not to say that the concerns we all have about the state of the world and our places in it are not real concerns. It's just that worrying doesn't resolve conflict or alleviate anxiety.

Take, for example, a television newscast reporting a senseless murder. The camera records the graphic elements of the crime scene, and the reporter chronicles the terrible suffering of the surviving family members. The story arouses a very powerful emotional response—compassion. Viewers feel sympathy for the family's sorrow as well as an impulse to change the tragedy in order to lessen their pain. Unfortunately, there is no way to change the fact that someone in the community has been murdered.

Compassion for the sadness of another turns to worry about issues of personal safety. What will prevent this tragedy from happening again? Is anyone safe from violence? When we react anxiously to images of violence on television, the reality of that violence does not change. **Worry alone doesn't add to real solutions, nor does it subtract from real problems. It is, in fact, a kind of optional suffering.**

Of course, worrying does have consequences, just not very effective ones. Prolonged, unchecked worry produces chemical responses in our bodies. Since the self is a body/mind/spirit composite, we feel worry on all levels. Anxiety blunts imagination and restricts optimism. It rouses fears that dissipate and diminish the energy needed for effective problem-solving at a time when we're trying to manage unwanted feelings.

Therefore, worry is not only nonproductive but also self-defeating. Our compassion for others demands that we seek to change those situations that cause suffering, in our lives as well as the lives of others in the human community. Dwelling on our inability to change the past robs us of the ability to live responsibly and realistically in the present and prevents us from seeing the possibility of change in the future. Anxiety affects our behavior and causes us to act irrationally. One way to combat it is with a reasonable strategy.

The good news is that each of us can use rationality to influence irrational behavior. We have hindsight to learn from the past, insight to see clearly the reality of the present, and foresight to imagine a better future. Our capacity to use these thought processes is limitless.

We etch inaccurate information into mental grooves when we store up unhelpful thoughts and act in an unreasonable manner. When we repeat the same thought or action, we deepen the groove. We establish a pattern. Soon, the pattern plays automatically, independently of our will or intention. It becomes a habit, and the burden of this pattern lies in the fact that we are actually operating automatically, without thinking. The pattern grows more automatic, more mindless, from sheer force of habit. The effect is of an unchecked inaccurate belief that lives in us as truth.

But remember that because we can form habits, we can also reform them. Reprogramming occurs when we subject both the course and practice of thinking, acting, and feeling to intentional change. We reform the grooves and replace them with new information not known, seen, or realized before. We can alter unhelpful thinking patterns when we recognize we want or need to change.

The first step in redirecting is to ask, "What happens now?" To reprogram that tiresome CD of useless worry and anxiety, you must begin in the present. The here-and-now is where change happens. You can most easily measure how much control you have over a given situation in the current moment.

Right now, each of us has the control necessary to end our worry. This doesn't mean that we have complete control over the situations and events that cause us to feel anxiety, although a rational response does allow us to influence the way changes happen in the world around us. We may control the effect those situations and events have on our lives by limiting the time we spend thinking and talking about them or things related to them. This involves changing a habit.

There are three basic processes that we must perform to exert personal influence over a well-established habit:

1. Replace the habit with another; or,
2. Modify or restructure the existing pattern to conform with new information; then,
3. Maintain the new pattern of thoughts and behaviors through practice.

None of these steps happen automatically; they require sustained personal efforts.

## Laying Down Your Burden, Feeling Your Energy Return

As you consider the processes that will allow you to change unhelpful thoughts and behaviors, it is valuable to imagine the size and shape of the habit. If the habit is worrying to excess about things you cannot control, assign the time and energy you spend on anxiety a weight, height, and width. If you were to carry your worry

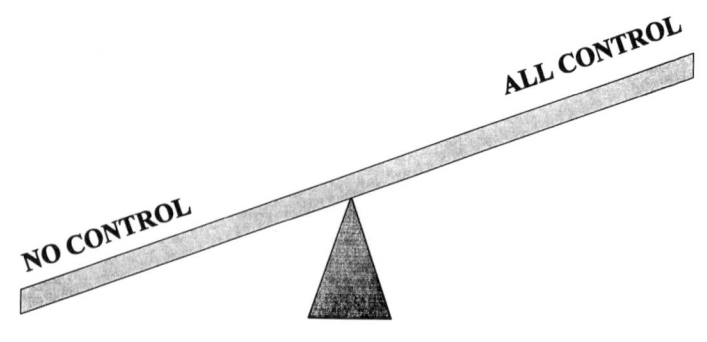

FIGURE 7-2

in your arms or on your back, could you manage it? Now, understand that this weight has been on your head.

Don't underestimate the power you'll feel once you lighten that load. Dropping that heavy burden of worry frees up the energy you used to maintain an unproductive habit. There will be plenty of mental, physical, and spiritual strength once you lay down your burden. (Energy is neither created nor destroyed—it is transformed. Redirecting your mental, physical, and soul energies is the task of this ingredient of change.)

The process of managing yourself by replacing, modifying, restructuring, and maintaining stirs your energy. The process of exploring new options, and then making and maintaining positive choices for change, heightens your awareness. The result is renewed energy for further exploration and productive choices.

## Getting Practical

The following exercises ask you to identify a thought or stream of thoughts that cause you distress, and to evaluate whether distress is a rational or irrational reaction.

## Exercise One: Change Formula

To train yourself for directing change, be aware of what's going on with you. Pain kicks off the cycle of change. This is what

gets your attention. To change of your own free will, you must be aware of:
- What you think
- How you feel
- What you're doing

*Step 1: Increase Awareness.* Describe in detail what happened, and what you thought and did in response.

*Step 2: Expand Options.* List several options you might have to change the situation.

*Step 3: Make Decisions or Choices.* Choosing is putting a decision into practice. Use the following to help you begin.

*I will start* _____.
*I will continue* _____.
*I will stop* _____.

### Exercise Two: The Problem of Worry (or Gaining Rational Control Over Irrational Interference)

Worry is one of many unhelpful mental habits. Worry is the unproductive torment of disturbing thoughts. It is keeping your fears on the front burner, filling you with anxious agitation.

Worry simply doesn't help. If you worry three more days besides the half day you have already worried, the outcome is still the same. That outcome is exhaustion. Worrying blunts your imagination and rouses your fears, robbing you of precious limited energy you need for effective problem solving.

That is the best reason to reduce the ineffective habit of worrying. It's a waste of time and energy. However, you do not change habits by labeling them as bad. Knowing that worrying is irrational is a start, but not enough to stop it.

Never underestimate the power of the first step of change: heightened awareness!

Keep notes about your worrying behaviors. Think about the following when you find yourself worrying:

My dog doesn't worry about the meaning of life. She will notice if she doesn't get her breakfast. But she doesn't worry about whether things are fair, or if she's raising her puppies properly. It's not her concern how much money there is in the checking account.

Make a list of your current worries. For example:

*Current Worry List*
1. Retirement (the future)
2. Not enough money
3.
4.
5.
6.

## Exercise Three: Reforming

Use the format in Figure 7-3 as a model for this exercise.

**REFORMING**

State the proposed change:

**List:**

| Advantages<br>Opportunities | Disadvantages<br>Costs |
|---|---|
| | |
| | |
| | |

FIGURE 7-3

## Exercise Four: Mind Stretching

Imagine what might happen if you were to lay down your burden. Now that you have let go, what next? Set your timer for ten minutes and start writing.

*Making Changes*

**IMAGINE!**

# 8
## PLANNING

*If anyone counts upon one day ahead or even more, he does not think. For there can be no tomorrow until we have safely passed the day that is still with us.*
—Sophicles, *The Women of Trachis*

*M*arie didn't know exactly what to change, but she knew something had to change. She gave Mark's treasured Volkswagen Beetle to the vo-tech school. It was very hard for her to do. Giving away his possessions made her realize that he really was gone. Afterward, she gave other of Mark's belongings to selected special people. Connecting with people in this small way helped Marie realize she needed to be alone less and that she didn't want to live in the midst of so many relics. She began to make regular lunch dates, and even went to an occasional movie.

Debbie, like Marie, had begun a new lifestyle. She started forging a new identity and redefining herself as a lesbian mom. Again like Marie, Debbie began asking what she needed, wanted, and didn't want. She began considering the options available to her. Should she live alone or with a partner? Whom should she tell about her lesbianism? When should she tell her sons? Should she "come out" at work?

Larry alternated between useful and useless activities. He admitted that he was drinking too much. He scheduled an appointment with a financial planner to reduce his anxiety about financial adjustments. A job employment group offered him realistic advice about his skills and options.

At the same time Larry was taking these productive steps, he had some less productive feelings. He thought about giving up and simply not working. His anger was apparent in his sarcastic and bitter treatment of colleagues, but he began to realize this use of his anger was a barrier to change.

The energy gained from the process of redirection can be exhilarating and uplifting. The sensation is close to that of flying. However, there is also a downside. Some of us have a fear of flying. Some of us need to feel the ground beneath us to feel safe. Nevertheless, no one can continue the process of change until the fear of the unknown is addressed. For this to happen, you must create a plan.

My friends Suzy and David, who are both psychologists, have a parrot named Bink. The bird has a limited but precise vocabulary. According to Suzy, the parrot's favorite words are, "Whaddaya scared of?" Bink asks this question about thirty times a day.

The bird's preference makes sense, because Suzy specializes in dealing with fear. She works in a clinic for people with anxiety and panic disorders. Fear is a favorite topic in Suzy's home.

Extreme anxiety and panic obviously interfere with the quality of the lives of the patients Suzy sees. However, the underlying fear that causes anxiety and panic is the most common barrier to productive change for her patients as well as the rest of us. Just like Bink, Suzy asks over and over each day, "Whaddaya scared of?"

The difference is that the parrot has no sense of the relevance of the question. He has no fear to keep him from taking flight if he escaped from his cage.

Ironically, Suzy had a very pronounced fear of flying. She always traveled by train. Her journeys to New York City to visit her parents took more time by rail, but the panic she felt just *thinking* about flying kept her from choosing air travel.

In her capacity as a therapist, Suzy was asked to facilitate a support group for fearful fliers. She accepted the challenge. Suzy explained to her group members that there are two kinds of fear. One is the fear that the plane will crash and the passengers will die. That's the fear of external catastrophe. The second is the fear of having a panic attack, which is fear of internal catastrophe. Fear is either specific or remote.

We all have fears, both real and imagined. The challenge is to adapt our behaviors and achieve balance in our lives, not to live without ever being scared. So Suzy's first question to her group members was "What are you scared of?" She asked them to name their fears, to prioritize what they were each most afraid of, and to make a written list of these items.

The next step was to develop a problem-solving plan that included matching appropriate educational and coping skills with an adaptive strategy. All planning involves creating a path to get from where you are to where you want to be.

The word educate comes from the Latin word *educare*, meaning "to lead." The group facilitator's role is to lead group members to an understanding of their own adaptive skills. With that understanding, they can experience more ease and less stress about a fear-provoking situation.

Suzy's plan for her fearful fliers was a typical cognitive-behavioral combination:

1. Practice relaxed breathing;
2. Identify thinking style;

3. Examine thoughts for accuracy;
4. Experiment with new behavior; and,
5. Evaluate the results.

This plan is one that clients can learn and practice; I have translated it into a recipe for a Cognitive Behavioral Therapy approach for dealing with fear.

## CBT Plan for Fear

*1. Practice relaxed breathing.* After naming their fears, people usually experience increased anxiety. Then, the fear is in control; breathing is rapid and shallow. This first step allows the person to reestablish control by taking charge of breathing, the most basic physical function. We learn better in a relaxed state, and it is difficult to breathe slowly and deeply while thinking fearful, anxious thoughts. So, we begin the plan for change by calming ourselves.

*2. Identify thinking style.* This step examines catastrophic thinking. You challenge your equivalent of the statement, I will crash and die if or when I fly. Thoughts contribute to feelings, which in turn affect behavior. The internal experience of emotional extremes (fear, anger, sadness, guilt) usually indicates you perceive some form of faulty thinking or mental inaccuracy as truth.

*3. Examine thoughts for accuracy.* Statistically, travel by air is one of the safest modes of transportation. In 1990, commercial airlines carried 466 million passengers; there were 39 fatalities. In that year more than 46,000 travelers died on the nation's roadways. Since travel by airplane is relatively safe, what evidence remains for the catastrophic belief? This step in planning allows the individual to replace the misperception with facts. The fear exists only in thought, not in reality. Label the statement, I will crash and die, as a thought and avoid thinking it. Remove it from your mind.

*4. Experiment with new behavior.* Instead of avoiding anxiety-producing situations, try exposure. The value of exposure therapy is to target personal coping skills and to build on them. This is where the hard work of therapy is done. Individuals move beyond merely thinking and talking about what should be changed. They begin a different course of action. Because this is an experiment, there is no pressure to perform perfectly without fear or shaking. The important lesson of exposure is that you do the very thing you fear doing and note what, if anything, occurs as a result of your actions.

**5. Evaluate results.** The final step, determining the results of the experiment, is reviewing specific information about the actual effects of the experiment. In other words, you monitor the results of experimenting with behaving differently and thinking differently. (Feelings will be the last to change.) You also observe your coping skills. All this information contributes to self-knowledge, and what you learn is not just a one-time lesson. Recycle that information and use it often.

Suzy's group of fearful fliers took a field trip to the Minneapolis/St. Paul International Airport as their exposure therapy. They confronted the symbol of their fear in the physical form of a DC-10 aircraft. They sat in the grounded plane as the chief pilot for Northwest Airlines presented a two-hour flight safety talk. The group members asked questions (checking their beliefs for accuracy) and openly discussed their concerns. Factual information replaced misperception, and they experienced sitting aboard an airplane without catastrophe.

At the clinic, group members learned more about cognitive restructuring. They reviewed their experiments and acquired pertinent cognitive-behavioral training. Group process and Suzy's facilitation reinforced that training. And Suzy conquered her own fear of flying. It's not surprising that some of us teach what we need to learn. There are fringe benefits in helping others solve problems.

I saw Suzy after she completed her facilitation of the fearful fliers group. I noticed a shift from fear to adaptation in her thinking. Suzy shared the change in her self-talk with me.

"When I used to dream of going someplace so far away I would need to fly," she said, "I struggled with my fear of flying by saying 'Just let me survive this one time.' Now I say, 'London would be a nice place to visit.'"

Suzy is now able to imagine herself en route to London by plane. She has replaced her goal of mere survival with one of enjoying freedom and enrichment. The achievement comes with developing a carefully considered plan of exposure to the fear source. This is followed by a process of thoughtful adaptation based on building the skills necessary to ensure the desired change.

## Devising and Revising a Plan for Change

Many of us realize that we want or need change in our lives. We aspire to making those changes happen. Every goal requires a plan for its achievement. The planning process includes:

1. **Aspiration:** What you want or need to change.
2. **Inspiration:** How the change will occur.
3. **Perspiration:** Making changes happen.

Even when the necessary components are all in place, you have to devise the plan so that you short-circuit your natural resistance to change. We all need to be aware of ourselves as the source of greatest resistance.

There are also external barriers that you must overcome. These barriers include all the forces of the status quo—institutional and interpersonal—that elevate the immediately familiar to a sacred position and reject anything new, different, or tried before unsuccessfully. To devise an effective plan, you will have to understand the barriers you must overcome. Following is a discussion of some of the most common barriers to change.

*1. Planning without practicality.* An impractical plan is doomed from the start. In a practical plan, the focus must be on the aspiration from the very beginning and throughout the process. What do you want or need to change?

Without a clear definition of the goal, one can imagine no practical plan to attain it. Following are self-talk statements and the underlying assumptions, all of which are examples of goals lacking clear definition. If you hear yourself making such statements, refocus on what you want or need to change.

| Self-Talk | Underlying Assumption |
| --- | --- |
| I don't deserve | I don't know where to start |
| I'm scared | What's the use |
| I might fail | What if so-and-so doesn't approve or agree |

**2. Planning by leaps and bounds.** Perhaps the single most important skill required for planned change is the ability to list and prioritize the steps necessary to reach the desired goal. The second most important skill is the ability to revise that list. This means planning for setbacks and unexpected occurrences along the way. Remain flexible about time. Don't be a prisoner to your plan.

When changing something significant in ourselves, we cannot think only of the entire project or we might never take the first step. While we want to have a vision of the big picture, good planning links that vision with reasonable consecutive steps. You don't have to accomplish the entire task all at once. In fact, to plan with such an impossible goal in mind is self-defeating.

**3. Planning with the wrong schedule.** Planning involves structuring time and using it wisely and effectively. When designing a schedule, consider two parts of change: the decision or intention and the process. The decision requires time for creating strategy; the process demands time for both accomplishment and maintenance. You will need time to think and time to act. Then you need time to reflect and possibly redirect. Part of the maintenance process is recycling past information and integrating positive thoughts. If you intend to schedule your time along a straight line, you will probably find your schedule very difficult to manage.

I find the concept and image of tacking to be useful. Tacking is a nautical term that refers to the zig-zag maneuvering used in sailing to get to a place when the wind is not blowing in that direction. Since you can't go directly into the wind, you have to head it off, gaining distance and speed by shifting your sails to starboard and port.

Tacking sacrifices the direct route for the sake of incremental moves which look like side steps. It calls for the skills of aligning yourself to the masterful and changing wind and using it to get where you want to go.

Remember that change is an ever-widening circle. Think about the model for redirecting energy in Chapter Seven: heighten awareness, expand options, make choices. Devising a plan for intentional change means articulating both intention and process.

The Getting Practical section of this chapter includes an exercise called Balancing Acts. It served as a guide for Larry and other clients I see who are facing job loss, relocation, or demotion due to corporate restructuring. The exercise also shows what a plan for intentional change might look like. Always build a variety of options and areas of familiarity for comfort (personal stability zones) into any change plan. Work with numbers; eight options are better than two—that's rainbow thinking.

This chapter started with an example of change planning related to the fear of flying. Certainly fear is a very debilitating emotion. It prevents people from doing what they want to do in their lives. There are other equally destructive emotions that keep individuals stuck in painful situations. Throughout this book I have identified those emotions as anger, sadness (grief), fear, and guilt. The change model uses the power of the individual's rational mind to combat the stagnating, resistant force of those emotions. The following example illustrates how a misperception of responsibility can lead to paralyzing guilt.

## Benign Delusion

Sarah's life fell apart three years ago. A couple had hired her to provide child care while they were away for a weekend.

After attending to the needs of the younger children, Sarah called for the sixteen-year-old son, since she hadn't seen him for a while. When he didn't answer, Sarah went looking for him. She found him lying on the bathroom floor. Apparently he had been there for some time; his skin was cold and blue. Sarah immediately summoned an ambulance, but help arrived too late. The paramedics could not revive the boy.

Sarah told this tragic story during one of the CBT groups I facilitate. She explained that the boy had been experimenting with inhalants to get high. He had been sniffing butane on the day he died, and the fumes had overcome him.

She clearly stated, and so was completely aware of, the circumstances of the teenager's death. The parents and siblings of the boy did not hold Sarah responsible for the tragedy in any way. In fact, the other children have been steadfast in their support of Sarah throughout the ordeal. There have been no criminal charges filed nor any legal action begun questioning her responsibility. Yet, Sarah believes that she is responsible. She alone casts blame.

There was a certain flatness of tone in the way Sarah told her story. She had told it so many times in the three years since the event that the words no longer affected her. The group thoughtfully reviewed the events as she told them, and pondered the issues of guilt and forgiveness. They noticed the discrepancy between the facts of the situation and Sarah's self-assessment. They questioned her perception that she was to blame, and suggested she was unreasonable in her assessment.

From the time the group first heard the story, they believed that Sarah had no responsibility for the boy's death. They couldn't understand why her perception was so very different from theirs. What the group didn't hear were the automatic thoughts spinning in Sarah's head. Without knowing those thoughts, there was no way to correct Sarah's situation.

Sarah's mental health picture was grim when she arrived in my group. She had been clinically depressed for two years, was actively suicidal, and was coping poorly with vegetative depressive symptoms. The onset of these symptoms was a personalized, false belief tied to a string of misperceptions. The depression started with a true statement: I was in charge when the boy died. There the facts ended and Sarah's misperception began. *I'm responsible, therefore I can't be trusted to do anything right,* followed by, *I have nothing to live for.*

She had to start at the beginning of the change process and question her paralyzed thinking. (Look back at Figure 1-2 in Chapter One and imagine Sarah's worksheet.)

At first, what Sarah said was true. Yes, she was babysitting. Yes, a child for whom she was providing care died. Remember that the power of black-and-white thinking exists because of initial truth. Missing from that truth, however, are all the various other factors that contributed to the death.

For instance, if Sarah had not been baby-sitting and someone else had been in the house instead, would the child still be alive? Would another baby-sitter have known the boy was experimenting with dangerous drugs in the bathroom? Or, would someone else have stood in the bathroom with the boy and watched his every move to ensure his safety? But then, what about the other children in the household? Is it possible that while standing guard over the sixteen-year-old boy, one of the younger, more vulnerable children might have fallen into harm's way? Where does the can of butane gas, the inhalant, figure into the truth? All Sarah saw was neglect, all she felt was guilt, because she was stuck in black-and-white thinking and blaming. She needed to consider the total reality of what occurred.

From the vantage point of alternative thinking, Sarah needed to deal with her resistance to seeing the boy's death as a situation over which she had no control. Her style of resistance, as described in Chapter Three, was sentencing.

The healing journey for Sarah was not about feeling good about herself immediately. She had to reenter the painful experience and expose herself to the source of her guilt. Only then could she release the inaccurate belief that she was responsible for the teenager's death and, therefore, not fit to live. As with many traumatic events, to heal one must revisit the time of the trauma.

Best efforts and hard work that is not guided by knowledge cannot secure truth. In this case, persisting in self-blame was unhelpful and was serving to keep Sarah stuck. Since no one could reveal new factual information to Sarah about the death of the boy, she needed to reexamine the knowledge that she had. The only possibility for changing Sarah's situation was in restructuring her incorrect belief about the event.

Earlier in the process of therapy, I asked Sarah what she knew about self-forgiveness. She said that she hadn't thought about forgiveness. I suggested she restructure her self-assessment, considering forgiveness. Sarah wanted to change. She just hadn't planned how to execute that change. The first step was to begin with awareness of what she needed to change. For Sarah, the journey in therapy was to move from self-condemnation to self-forgiveness. She started at the point where she was stuck and agreed to consider the idea that she was not guilty of causing the boy's death. This was the change process for which she made a plan.

## Getting Practical
### Exercise One: Balancing Acts

As we've discussed, change is not an option—only how you change is an option. This exercise is designed to help people deal with organizational change, but the principles are valid for many other applications.

1. Decide what you have control over and what you do not. Let go of what you can't change. Take charge in areas you have control.
2. Take personal responsibility for your pace of life and for major life changes.
3. Maintain a foundation of sound health and fitness.
   - Exercise is a natural stress reliever.
   - Relaxation is important in managing stress.
   - Distraction from pressures helps control anxiety.
4. Find and use ways to express feelings (frustration, anger, sadness, helplessness, impatience, irritation, excitement). Make choices about which way is the most profitable for you to do this.
5. Assess your ability to listen to and absorb rumors, gossip, and complaining. Decide what limits you will set regarding this type of input.
6. Create or keep a strong, stable support group of family and friends.
7. Seek counseling or professional help with job issues. Help can come from a colleague, a friend, or employee assistance.

**INFORMAL** ←————————————→ **FORMAL**
FRIENDS•BOOKS•JOB GROUPS•SEMINARS•INFORMATION INTERVIEWS•EAP HEALTH

FIGURE 8-2

←————————————→
PERSONAL RELATIONSHIPS•CHURCH•ASSOCIATIONS*•VACATIONS•GROUPS•
SHOPPING
SOFTBALL LEAGUES*
FISHING GROUPS*
CARD CLUBS*

FIGURE 8-3

8. Cultivate patience with imperfection—in yourself, in others, and in systems.
9. Create and maintain personal stability zones.
10. Explore the other side of change and possibly make decisions in your best interest. Make written lists of the pros and cons.
11. Recognize you are not your job. Consciously separate your identities and your professional and personal spaces. Leave your work at the office or work space.
12. Keep humor and perspective a part of your life.

Change is always accompanied by loss of the familiar as well as the opportunity to gain something different and better. It is important to recognize the losses and mourn them as part of the cycle.

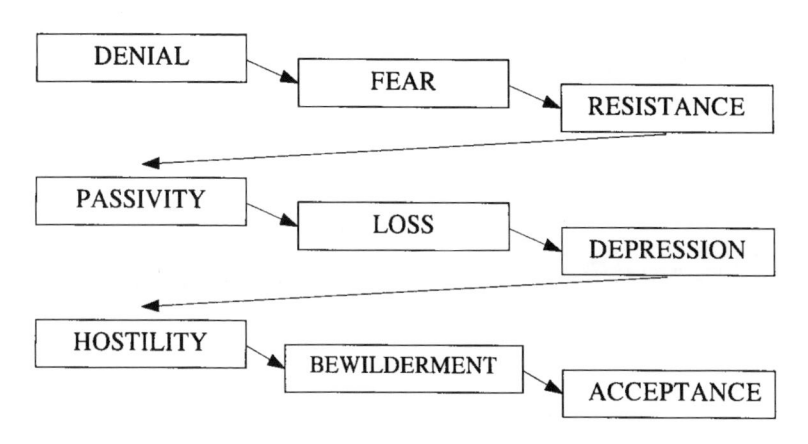

```
DENIAL → FEAR → RESISTANCE
         ↙
PASSIVITY → LOSS → DEPRESSION
         ↙
HOSTILITY → BEWILDERMENT → ACCEPTANCE
```

FIGURE 8-4—PIECES OF CHANGE

*Accommodating*

# 9

## CHOOSING

*M*arie decided to carry on with her life. Months dragged by, filled with what seemed like unspeakable agony. It was hard for her to notice any difference between one week and the next. She lost interest in everything. Nothing held much meaning for her.

People grieve as uniquely as they love. Marie made a deliberate choice about her grieving process when she returned to Elderhostel at St. Olaf College in Northfield, Minnesota, in 1992. She had hoped her son Mark would attend St. Olaf and had eagerly taken him to visit the beautiful campus in 1979. Following high school during the summer of 1980, Mark took theater classes at St. Olaf. Marie attended Elderhostle classes there so she could visit him and see his work.

Seven years after his death, Marie returned to St. Olaf Elderhostle. She registered for a class in short story-writing, and found herself writing about Mark's death. In her stoic way, Marie chose to stay connected to her self by incorporating her grief into her creative work. Her story ends, "On August 18, 1986, Mark died from an aortic rupture associated with Marfan's Syndrome. Mark, I miss you."

Small steps seem much larger when they bring you out of the kind of darkness Marie experienced. Marie's choice to revisit where she *knew Mark's memories would stir was a step toward resuming her life. Beginning to socialize again and speaking publicly of Mark's death were other small steps for this woman of few words. Marie chose to continue taking small steps toward an uncharted life she never dreamed she would be living.*

## THE PROCESS OF DECIDING

Decisions are what change our lives. Choosing becomes a decision point when you realize you could be serving yourself in a better way. It is revaluing reality over illusion, present over past, freedom over rice.

From what source does this ability to decide in your own best interests derive? In part, the ability comes from paying attention to your pain. Another piece is the ability to determine when the pain of one choice outweighs that of another. Shifting perspective after gathering and weighing all the information available is important. Finally, effective decision making comes from knowing you are the one identifying your needs and wants.

We all learn patterns of thinking and behaving to adapt and survive. We first developed and maintained those patterns because they served a function. When a time comes that the usual and practiced way of functioning no longer serves, it is time for a change of strategy. You must make a different choice. Personal dissatisfaction may indicate that your usual patterns of thinking, observing, noting, and deciding are not getting you what you want or where you want to be.

We realize the old way of being no longer serves. The pain of continuing in the old way is greater than the risk of trying a different way—it outweighs the risk of choosing differently. We choose with the hope that the choice we make will serve our purpose in a different and less painful way.

This is a decision point. We realize there is no one to decide for us. There is no one to rescue us from facing this choosing time.

In therapy sessions, we take time to reflect about these matters. In the process of questioning and conversing, new information comes forth, and clients heighten their awareness. New information may come from reality checks with others, CBT exercises, or by lifting up to a conscious awareness what was previously not conscious.

While therapists collaborate with clients and encourage awareness of new information, we cannot (nor can anyone) make their choices for them.

When Debbie told her husband about her choice to be known as a lesbian, he was furious and demanded she leave their home immediately. Her primary choice necessitated other, unwanted choices, such as leaving her spouse, sons, and home. She hadn't planned to move so abruptly, but knew she couldn't remain under the circumstances. The first weeks were extremely stressful. When her therapist suggested she join a lesbian mom's support group, she did so. She enjoyed support from women with similar challenges.

## Basic Stress Management Tools

Deciding to change is stressful. Learning new ways of dealing with situations simply creates anxiety. There is no benefit in having a hundred stress management tools if you don't use them. My approach to managing stress is simplify, simplify, simplify. You can manage the stress of change with a few basic tools, just as you can manage your home with a few maintenance tools. Less can be more effective in the long run. The secret is in just doing it.

Chapter Twelve deals more extensively with stress management. For now, these six Stress Smarts cover most of the bases:

1. Think differently
2. Express yourself
3. Meditate
4. Engage in physical exercise
5. Watch proper nutrition
6. Do something about the source of stress

Choosing involves selection. Choosing is tantamount to your singular vote shifting the direction of what follows. By choosing, you declare, Here's what it's going to be. Even though Debbie struggled with what others would think of her and her choice, she decided to leave her marriage. Even following her lifestyle change, she continued her old pattern of seeking too much approval from others. Debbie's major lifestyle change drew outright disapproval from the most important people in her life. Despite her fears, she chose to validate herself in an authentic way by remaining true to her self and her choice. In doing so, she shifted the value of approval from the most important people in her life—her spouse, her children, her mother.

Sometimes choosing to respond to old pain in a new way is the only chance to alleviate optional suffering. Often our choices mean again facing these core themes (competency, control, belonging, acceptance) as we have before in the process of change. Our identity is sometimes disrupted by events and issues having to do with these themes. We are face-to-face with the question, "Who am I now?" Choosing to shift the importance of your personal value involves weighing costs and gains. Authentic choice, even a tiny shift from a previous stance, creates a change.

When Larry had limited time to choose between being laid off or assuming a scaled down position, he decided to accept the unattractive position with his same company. Larry really didn't like either of these options, yet he chose the more stable. Given these circumstances, Larry made a few other immediate decisions. He realized his angry and bitter attitude was hurting him, and he decided he wanted to feel better. He had a vague sense that he needed to diversify and broaden his life, but he didn't really know what that meant. He allowed himself time to think about the options. Months later, he made some other choices.

There comes a time when you choose to change the way you burn your energy, whether mental, physical, or spiritual. If you're looking for a well-marked highway, you may miss the turn. The proverbial fork in the road may require only a small step onto one path or the other.

Larry's willingness to let himself think about his options moved him into the next step of change, rainbow thinking. I use this tool to help clients avoid paralyzed thinking and polarized choices.

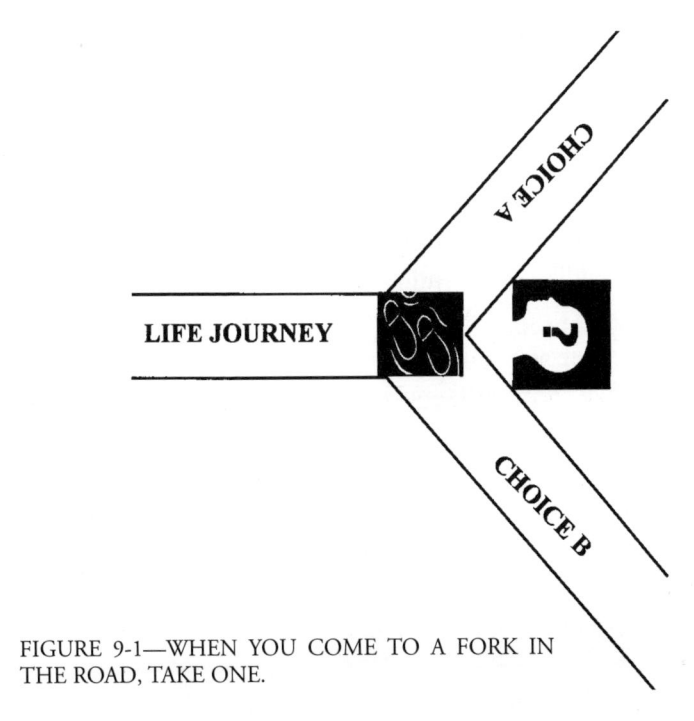

FIGURE 9-1—WHEN YOU COME TO A FORK IN THE ROAD, TAKE ONE.

Larry's choices were to stay or to leave. For Larry, rainbow thinking might have included deciding to stay for a time, with a less destructive attitude. He could have stayed while considering better stress management, pursuing hobbies, developing leisure time, or contemplating a job hunt.

Choosing is different from becoming resigned or powerless. When choosing, you select how you will direct your thinking and

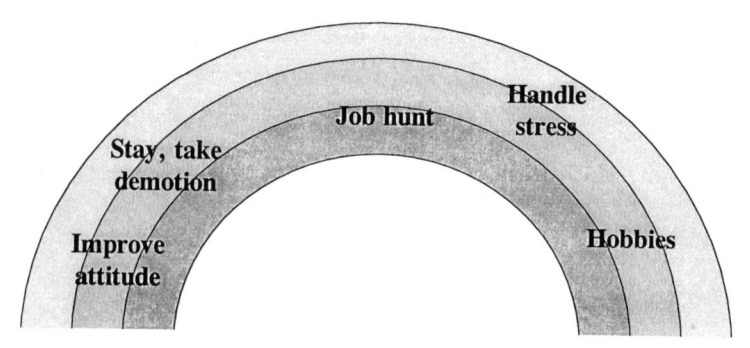

FIGURE 9-2

behavior. It is crucial to select the attitude you want to live with, especially in the face of unwanted change that involves your soul.

We do not become powerless in the face of unwanted change. We still think something, do something, feel something. Feelings are usually the last thing to change. They are based on what we think and how we interpret events. Sometimes changing feelings is as simple as accurate naming.

Language not only makes thought apparent, but also enhances the power to make changes. CBT uses the power of written language to channel energy to change experience and to record those changes. Language is a tool to clarify thinking and develop precision meaning. Consider the difference between "I can't do it" and "I don't know how." Language reflects what you mean.

Consider the implied meanings of these statements:
- They made me do it…
- You make me feel…
- I shouldn't be this way.
- I never do anything right.
- You always…
- I ought to…
- Let's get together sometime.

What do these statements name? They name nothing, but they do generalize and blame. The importance of naming is finding the truth. When you say something accurately, you capture the truth. This truth has consequences.

The truth is you feel, you will, you want, you choose, you act. When you assign the action to someone else, you lose your power because you have made that person responsible for you. When you are the actor, you claim your thinking, feeling, wanting, willing, and acting as the substance of your choices. This is what makes personal choice. Accurate language heightens your awareness of this possibility. Precision and truth are found in the nuances and detail of reality. A seemingly slight shift provides focus and heightens awareness.

## Effective Thought Replacements

Clients work hard to shift their thinking. When a statement grasps the idea, it's important to save it. I keep a file of Effective Thought Replacements (ETRs) to draw upon. These statements can channel your thinking, ground you in your focus, and give you pep. Think of them as mental snacks. Training yourself to speak accurately is a way of reducing the stress of change.

Following are a few examples of ETRs you can use to start your own file:

- If I don't change my language, I can't change my thinking.

- Because I didn't receive love from my mother doesn't mean I can't enjoy loving.

- I don't say 'I can't stand it' when I am standing it.

- Only I can stop worrying.

- I can't live tomorrow today.

- Clarity is intellectual morality.

- Gray is the way (good for polarized thinkers).

- I can't move time, but I can direct the time I have.

- I can't just keep breathing out.

- I need a seed to get started.

- I have to trust myself before I can trust anyone else.

- The mistake I made was seeing the edge of the rut as my horizon.

- Some people will be there for me and some will not.

- Nobody gets everything they need, or thinks they need.

- Starting doesn't ever stop.

- When I see how I contribute to the problem, I can see how I contribute to the solution.

- I am doing something to leave footprints.

- I can get home to myself by way of music, forest, ocean, sunrise, solitude, massage, and good food.

- Live the truth in love.

## Getting Practical
### Exercise One: Articulating Goals—Naming Is Transition

Stating your truth is a good way of keeping promises to yourself. This is the basis of personal ethics. If I am not true to my word, then how can I trust anyone else to be true to theirs? As we all know, talking is easier than doing. However, writing intentions increases the odds of follow-through. Writing is also a way of being accountable to yourself. Making your list of intentions visual may bring a lump to your throat. It's an act of commitment.

Using the following examples for inspiration, write some of the rules by which you currently live.

*1994 resolutions*
1. Ask for help
2. Choose my battles
3. Moisturize and stretch
4. Slow down
5. Drink more water
6. Plan my future

*Another set of rules a friend offered*
1. Eat whole food
2. Play hard, work hard
3. Reciprocate friendships

*Marie's list on her seventy-second birthday*
1. Keep active
2. Get exercise
3. Don't be overweight—it's hard on my knees

Keep in mind your three essential parts (mind/body/spirit) and address all three as you write your rules.

*Choosing*

## Exercise Two: Turning Points

There is something encouraging about a fresh start. I ritualize starting anew by setting down a few guidelines to set the direction for the new beginning. This is a way of raising awareness and setting the tone by weaving a little of the previous cycle into the new one.

New beginnings have been a favorite part of my history since my teaching days. January 1 always fell during vacation and just a few days before my birthday. Kicking off the new year with some reflection and a few resolutions has long been my practice. Such times offer an opportunity for reflecting on and planning for the business of recycling.

Turning points are decision points. Think about some of your experiences with the following. Then write some thoughts and feelings about them.

- Something I have quit…
- Something I continue to do for myself…
- Something I have joined and continue membership in…
- A cause I contribute money to…
- Other…

## Exercise Three: S.M.A.R.T. Change

Use the format in Figure 9-4 on the following page to set up a worksheet for your plan for change. Keep your completed worksheet with a planning calendar you use to schedule target dates and track your progress.

## S.M.A.R.T.* CHANGE WORKSHEET

I, _____ [your name], intend to make this change for myself:
_____ [change].

I plan to accomplish this by _____ [date].

Here's how I'll do it [list actions in appropriate categories]:

| MIND | BODY | SPIRIT |
|---|---|---|
| 1 _____ | 1 _____ | 1 _____ |
| 2 _____ | 2 _____ | 2 _____ |
| 3 _____ | 3 _____ | 3 _____ |

I'll encourage and reward myself by:

1 _____
2 _____
3 _____
4 _____

[Attach calendar with target dates marked]

\*
| |
|---|
| **S** <br> Start with the end specifically in mind. |
| **M** <br> Measure—use numbers. |
| **A** <br> Attainable—"do-able." |
| **R** <br> Rewards—logically connected and relevant. |
| **T** <br> Time binds—set dates; Track and monitor actions. |

FIGURE 9-4

# 10
## PRACTICING

*Knowing doesn't happen all at once. You have to grow into it. So, some days I walk on water, some days I nearly drown.*

$\mathcal{M}$*arie practiced* not *being in denial. Her grief was still strong, and she stayed alive to her grief. She did things she thought Mark and her husband would do if they were with her. When Mark's favorite Dixieland banjo band played at the Ordway, she took a long nap in the afternoon and went to the concert that evening. She had a blast. Later, she bequeathed her husband's and son's musical instruments to her niece.*

*Debbie began acting consistently with her new identity, accepting the outcomes of her choices. She began dating, attended a lesbian mom's group meetings, and began to learn about her new lifestyle. Trying to honor her new sense of authenticity, she frequently took time to stay in touch with herself. She debated with herself about telling more people at work about these changes. She struggled with her divorce process. Balancing the stress of adopting a new lifestyle with maintaining her responsibilities as head of the department was a challenge.*

*Larry stopped several habits that were not helping his situation. He stopped spending so much time at work, avoided gripe sessions with other displaced workers, stopped comparing himself with others, and decreased his alcohol consumption. He balanced his life by increasing time in his woodworking shop, reading want ads, and networking with other managers across the city. Talking during the job group sessions defused his anger and created small shifts in his attitude so he felt less victimized. He began focusing more on the future than on the past.*

## LIFE AS JOURNEY

I see life as a journey. Each person begins at a certain time. We call that the beginning. It is a tiny start, beginning with a single cell. This is the humble beginning of the self. We are certain to have an end, although there are different theories about what happens to the self after life as we know it. For the sake of this discussion, we'll refer to the end as death.

Every journey has a beginning and an end. What happens along the way is the adventure part. What amazes me is that no two journeys are exactly alike. Every self is unique. Each of us gets specific gear. Some gear we inherit with our genes. Some we accumulate through our particular experience. There is just no arguing with the fact that who and where we come from contribute to each of us being totally unique.

In a way, we are who we are from the time we are a seed to the time we stop being a living, breathing self. Yet, we are not whole and complete at any point along the way. The journey of becoming a self is a process. Our journey occurs in and over time.

From beginning to end, there are two constants: self and change. The ability to change is the skill we need from birth to death. How have we learned how to change? Who taught us how to change?

## Journey As Destination

More and more I've been thinking of the journey as the destination as well. None of us has any guarantees about what will happen along the way.

Change is more difficult than we realize. That's why practice is so necessary. Without practice, we fail to strengthen the new attitudes, actions, and feelings that reinforce the desired change.

Anyone can practice. Even after you have decided upon and developed a plan, implementing your plan for change requires persistence. Practice also requires persistence. Practice makes what is new become familiar. At first, new thinking will seem awkward. You may need to fine tune new thinking as you would tune a radio that loses clear reception.

It is helpful to have one interest or discipline you stay with under all circumstances. Having a commitment to someone or something provides you a certainty on which you can rely. Practicing is a way of valuing. Whatever you practice—whether you choose running, parenting, writing, or any other interest—you add to your bank of experience.

You build trust by practicing. There is no other way to build stamina and muscle. Tenacity comes with practice. Practice means you stick with your original commitment. You do what you say you will do, regardless of circumstances, come rain or come shine.

Practice involves repetition; sticking with something for the sake of getting better at it. Getting surer, better, stronger is the "sweaty" part of commitment to yourself and your choices.

Practicing also involves intangible items, such as will and self-discipline. In fact, self-discipline and practicing are linked—it takes self-discipline to practice. Not only do we need to "just do it," we need to include our mind/body/spirit in doing it. Practicing involves not only steering toward your intended direction but also keeping alert for snags or distractions on your course.

Whether we like it or not, the process of trial and error is how we learn new proficiencies. Even geniuses experience repeated tumbles and falls. We all learn from experience. If we don't make mistakes, we don't discover what works. Even more important, we don't discover what doesn't work. When you practice, you become stronger and more sure of yourself through the ups and downs of it.

You must expect to miss the mark sometimes. The roots of familiarity want to maintain their stranglehold on your behavior. Besides, life is a process of continually switching to plan B. Learning to understand how we slip is part of integrating mistakes, and it's how we avoid repeating the same ones over and over. This is essential to good practice. Beware of judging yourself in this practicing phase for not being good enough, fast enough, smart enough, or just not enough.

## The Strategy of Hitting Singles

Practicing is a small word but a big concept. Practicing is an ingredient of change that allows small, manageable moves to amount to a big difference over time. The first step is the one on which all other steps depend, so naturally it is often the hardest.

Take comfort measures, even if you have to force yourself. Group therapy is an opportunity to take time to talk with others, and such communication can be one of the greatest comforts anyone can have.

As another comfort strategy, try for a moment to turn off all thoughts in your mind. Mind is more than brain. The functioning of mind is an involuntary phenomenon, like that of our heart and lungs. We do, however, have some control over the condition of our organs through exercise and nutrition. In much the same way, we can enhance our mind control with practice. I recommend this practice for stilling yourself and observing things just the way they are. It's a practice in watching reality just as it is.

The rules we practice in the CBT group sessions are all very useful for developing mind control. They are:
- Keep breathing.
- Remember we are mind/body/spirit beings.
- Tell your truth.
- Keep confidences.
- Be present.
- Take comfort even if you have to force yourself.

One way to enhance your mind's control is to use breathing. *Keep breathing* is the first rule in the CBT groups I facilitate for a good reason. We begin each group session with breathing. I teach a three-step method of quieting the mind so that fear and other emotions do not interrupt.

1. Sit comfortably erect, hands cupped gently in your lap with palms up. Focus your eyes on a spot on the floor, or close them.
2. Breathe deeply and slowly. Lengthen your breath as much as you can.
3. Practice just observing your mind. Let thoughts simply pass through your mind. Don't try to bring thoughts or push them away.

This calming practice is a passive activity. You experience allowing everything to be the way it is. For many, these are rare moments of silence. Quieting mental interference is a skill that improves with practice, but there is no substitute for this experience. One must do it to have it.

I've witnessed the power of practicing during the past ten years in the Stress & Depression Management Center of Fairview Riverside Medical Center. This power is proof that a force resides within our mind/body/spirit being, with heavy emphasis on mind. (We are still indivisible as a bubble even when singling out one of the three.)

Our mind is always working. Our brain is always thinking, but our thoughts are not always accurate. We discover a great deal when we pay closer attention to how the mind works. We see connections, errors, and reality.

Part of practicing is living by your rules and trusting your sense of direction. Presenting on the outside what is inside is only possible *if you live by your rules*. Writing helps develop new mind skills. We must see what *is* before we can imagine what *could be* and choose what *will be*. Practicing persistently, using repetition, and continually refining are part of the education process Jung spoke of in molding a new habit:

We seldom get rid of an evil by understanding its causes. And for all our insight, obstinate habits do not disappear until replaced by other habits. Habits are won by exercise, and appropriate education is the sole means to this end. No amount of confession and no amount of explaining can make the crooked plant grow straight; it must be trained upon the trellis.

*Marie is a study in perseverance. She has endured losses at levels she was unable to comprehend. The loss she suffered when her twenty-six-year-old son collapsed from a hemorrhage was totally unexpected. She had planned for good health for her family in the future. They had been to all the right physicians. She had been more than diligent in tending to Mark's symptoms: flat feet, arched palate, sticky skin, spinal curvature, and ocular problems.*

*She moved through the shock of loss. The wake and funeral motivated her to keep functioning through the initial shock. An inner energy sustained her efforts. Some call this faith. But no matter what it's called, it's an inner strength and perspective born of suffering.*

*Debbie redefined herself at core levels. She didn't have enough experience to know whether she met the requirements of being a lesbian. She reevaluated the values that had always guided her. She began revising herself as she went along. Debbie executed a mathematical exchange by dropping an established identity and adding different identity parts she didn't have before. She has experienced a new definition of herself since she shed her old identity as a married, heterosexual mother of twin boys. When Debbie found herself emotionally involved with a married woman, she definitely felt confused. She thought to herself, How can this be? It goes against everything I grew up with.*

*Larry is someone who gave his all for a clearly identified goal, only to discover that someone moved the goal posts. The criteria for success changed without his knowledge or consent. He also has had to begin creating a new identity based on something other than his job.*

In my practice of psychotherapy, I hear many good lines. A well-stated phrase can guide your thoughts, feelings, or actions in any given direction. The following statements of reform, reinforcement, and replacement help you learn to think differently. They help you to name and practice new ways of thinking.

### TIPS ON PRACTICING CHANGE

- You are the best person to manage your self change.
- Pace yourself as you change.
- Keep a small blank book handy to write the changes as they occur. Note what you want to change, what has worked in the past, or good ideas and lines you think of or hear.
- Every change means good-bye to one thing and hello to another.
- When you try a new change, set it up for one week. Then review. Planned changes fail most often for want of a review.
- Inform those around you what you are changing. Ask for their help. "I'm walking ten minutes every day during lunch. Want to join me?"
- Write some of your options for change into columns headed *What I Can Change, What I Can't Change,* and *What I Won't Change.*

- Work at letting go of what you can't change.
- Allow yourself to have your feelings about your change process.
- Select a favorite phrase, song, or poem that helps you use your energy the way you want.
- Keep a procrastination list headed Things I Am Putting Off Doing. Follow it with two ongoing lists: Why I Want To and Why I Don't Want To.
- If you believe you can change, you can. If you believe you can't change, you won't.
- Write self-sticking notes to yourself and put them anywhere and everywhere, reinforcing your resolve.
- Avoid comparing your progress to what, how much, and how easily others seem to change.
- Remember things are not always what they seem.
- Always allow heroes to inspire you.
- Remember that changes don't have to cost more money.
- A big mistake with changing is thinking you can't.
- Just to keep your wheels greased, do one small thing you've never done before. Take a bus, eat a new food, see a movie alone. Observe yourself. Write your responses in your Journey Notes.
- For a change, go shopping and buy nothing.
- Tell someone a mistake you've made recently. Give details. Make a short story of it. After you've told the story of your latest mistake, end by completing this sentence: The meaning of this mistake story is…
- Change is a combination of heightening self-awareness, expanding options, and making choices. How many times do you estimate you do this in a given day?
- Change is fundamentally stopping or starting something. Between these two options is a neutral space,

like the slight pause between inhaling and exhaling. Do not be surprised if, when you are in this neutral place, you feel as if you are hanging in midair. In a way, that's exactly what is happening. Know that it, too, is a part of the cycle of change. Try to expand your tolerance for discomfort to include the necessity of some insecurity.
- The biggest mistake with changing is trying to change someone else.
- Get to know your style of changing. Especially become familiar with your style of letting go and making choices. Dropping and adding are basic moves of change.

**Two sure-fire ways to fail:**

**1 Do nothing**
**2 Keep doing what's not working**

FIGURE 10-1

## Change Is Not An Option; Only How You Change Is An Option

I want to speak personally here about this business of practice. You see, I didn't really plan to write this book. My clients and students requested copies of the training material I was using. So I simply thought I would just write it in a book.

In July of l989, I attended the Split Rock Arts Program in Duluth, Minnesota. The five-day course was "How to Write a Book Proposal." The original title of this book, *How Do You Learn What You Need to Know for the Journey You Hadn't Planned to Take?*, summarized three ideas I wanted to expand:

- How do we know what we know?
- How do we plan for the unknown?
- Life is a journey.

Reflecting on the process since then, I realize how terribly naive I was—specifically, in tackling a very large project without a plan. My experiences since beginning this book have stretched me in many ways. I have complained about loneliness and isolation, hosted fears of both failure and accomplishment. I've felt both stupid and smart. I have neglected responsibilities for my home, family, friends, and health. I have practiced what I preach by portioning out small comforts to compensate for the hardships. I have woven unwanted changes of my own into the text of Making Changes. This is truly the most consuming and difficult task I have ever undertaken. Anything you do fully brings you face to face with yourself. When you go deeply into a thing, you find it is connected to everything.

*"Nothing in the world can take the place of persistence. Talent will not; nothing is more common than unsuccessful men with talent. Genius will not; unrewarded genius is almost a proverb. Education will not; the world is full of educated derelicts. Persistence and determination alone are omnipotent. The slogan 'Press On' has solved and always will solve the problems of the human race."* —Anonymous

The quality of trust grows through practice. I trust people who practice. I like what experience shows, that I can do it. How do I know I can write? Practicing is proof that I can write. I am writing, that's how I know. I can call myself a writer if I'm burning my energy writing.

> **EFFECTIVE THOUGHT REPLACEMENTS**
>
> I love my creative life more than I love cooperating with my own oppression.
>
> •
>
> I am doing something to leave footprints.
>
> •
>
> I can get home to myself by way of music, forest, ocean, sunrise, solitude, massage, good food.
>
> FIGURE 10-2

## The Economy of One Liners

In our age of information overload, our beings revel in simplicity. "So, do you think there will be a Kuwaiti restaurant on every other corner after the Gulf War?" When I first heard this on a late night comedy routine, my mind ping-ponged back and forth. I could almost cry and laugh at once. There are so many truths in that one line.

Comedians cause us to think a certain way. They grab our minds and shake them around so we see things from a different angle. A good line is like a cartoon. It gets through fast, makes contact, then simmers with reverberating meanings. You get a lot with a little.

Those who lean way too far in the direction of focusing on others pay the price of short changing self. We all live with limited resources. The most common complaints I have heard from women and men in the last ten years are: I don't know who I am. I care too much about others. I don't care enough about myself.

Untangling the roots of that imbalance nearly always leads back to the Golden Rule. Taken at face value, this is a rule to live by. It's about fundamental fairness, giving and taking with some kind of balance.

## Getting Practical
### Exercise One: Making Corrections

My father loved sports. He taught me how to throw and catch. "Two hands while you're learning," he'd say when I tried one-handed catches before I mastered keeping the ball in my glove.

Reflect on and write about how you encourage yourself when you drop the ball or miss the mark. What is your practice for making corrections?

### Exercise Two: Thinking Allowed

Practice writing your thoughts about yourself. Use the following to help you start:
- What helps my mind run clear…
- I remember…
- I don't remember…
- I'm thinking of a symbol…
- I've always had trouble…
- I know…
- I don't know…

### Exercise Three: Discarding

Reviewing your gear is like cleaning out a closet. You set some time aside to dig into the mess. You discover things buried there you didn't know you kept. It is an opportunity to assess and reassess what to do with things. Some items may have been meaningful at some time, but aren't any longer. You may have outgrown some items. Some things have outlived their usefulness. Discarding is an exercise in letting go of what you no longer need.

1. Write your thoughts and feelings about something you want to discard.
2. Write your thoughts and feelings about something you have discarded and are glad you did.

3. Write your thoughts and feelings about some nuance of discarding.

# 11
## SELFING

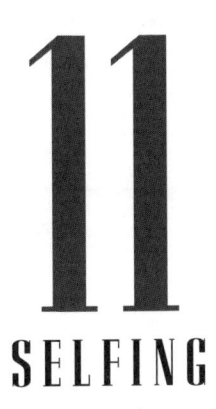

*We can't all reach our goals and win, but we can—each of us—set our goals and accomplish what we set out to do. And that's winning, too.*

*Marie commented, "I don't choose hard things, but hard things choose me." She preferred to pursue compassion rather than bitterness. Living as a single woman at the age of seventy was not something she had ever wanted. Once she had to, however, she began to do more than she'd ever allowed herself to do in the past. Awareness of limited time focused her priorities. She committed to focusing on her needs and wants, and to living more fully. In an intentional effort to extend compassion to others she volunteered at the homeless center and worked with local refugee families.*

*Selfing for Debbie included a recognition of her impulsive patterns. She decided she wanted to communicate more honestly in her relationships, and developed finer discrimination about her wants and* needs. She acknowledged her tendencies to avoid conflict due to fear of disapproval, and realized what a barrier her fear was. She revalued staying in touch with herself. She wished she had taken more time to process during the years of confusion and withholding, as well as the last year of her marriage.

Larry realized the job demotion greatly affected his self-esteem, and he was forced to think more clearly about who he was, with or without the job. He began to identify other things he liked about himself—his sense of fair play and hard work, his parenting, his artistic interests. He began to revalue relationships, starting with his relationship with himself. From there he began to connect more with his children.

Self is the fundamental agent of change. And selfing is:
- Using your own voice, saying what you have to say.
- Thinking for yourself, here and now.
- A special kind of claiming that says "I'm talking now."

> At another time she asked, "What is a soul?" "No one knows," I replied; but we know it is not the body, and it is that part of us which thinks and loves and hopes...and is invisible..." "But if I write what my soul thinks," she said, "then it will be visible, and the words will be its body."
>
> —Helen Keller to Annie Sullivan, 1891

FIGURE 11-1

- Steering yourself in the direction you want to go.
- It includes accepting the consequences of your actions.

Essentially, the act of selfing is to persist in the process of personal definition despite all resistance, using whatever life hands you. Selfing is saying what you want to say, using your own voice, thinking your own thoughts, and acting in your own best interest.

Selfing is the experiential accumulation of all the ingredients of change: questioning, hurting, struggling, clarifying, claiming, releasing, redirecting, planning, choosing, practicing, and recycling. Selfing as the eleventh step in the change cycle embodies elements of the other ingredients. That's what makes selfing a gerund, or "-ing" word. If there is no breathing, there is no breath. Selfing is like breathing and breath; there can't be one without the other.

Selfing is the steady insertion of your being into the world. It is the steadfast assertion that your being—who you are—is unique and distinct from all others. Selfing is the realization that no matter what the current situation, an inner-directed life is possible and preferable to a life led without self-knowledge.

Selfing describes the process of authentic change, change from the inside out. The inner self practices change, using experience and reexamining the meaning there. Selfing is developing unique patterns of thinking, feeling, and acting—patterns that are tailored to fit the needs of each individual. The process of selfing and all the thoughts, feelings, and actions associated with it requires that each of us define our individual self. Each of us decides what is self and what is not.

## Finding Self

When beginning counseling, many of my clients say, "I don't know who I am. I've given myself away (to my kids, my partner, my job)." Although these clients say they no longer exist as separate and distinct selves, the truth is they have merely devoted too

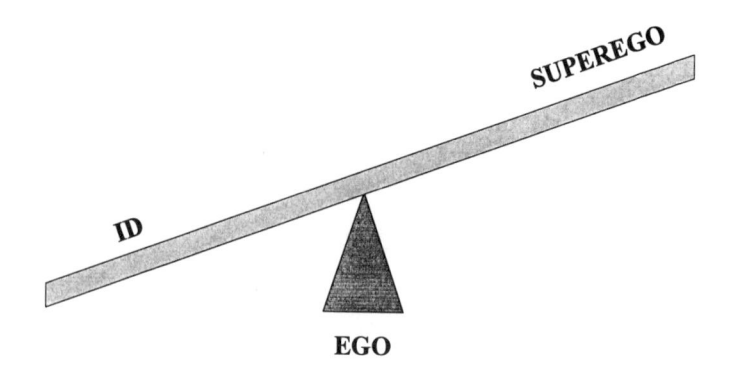

*(Diagram: a teeter-totter with ID on the low left, SUPEREGO on the high right, balanced on EGO.)*

much time and energy to the welfare of the external world. They have paid too little attention to their inner lives.

There are so many confusing messages about who we should be and how we should behave that we place too much focus on external realities, and often just the intangibles. (External intangibles include things like the self-sacrifice of parents and the fidelity of partners.) A deficiency in the amount of energy we use to manage matters of the inner world, a lessening of self focus, results. Remember from Chapter One that imbalance (excess and deficiency) is at the root of pain—physical, emotional, and spiritual.

This concept of imbalance is at the heart of modern psychology. Freud saw psychological balance as a teeter-totter:

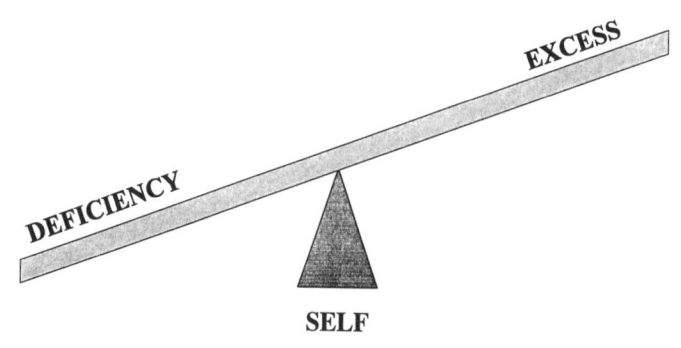

*(Diagram: a teeter-totter with DEFICIENCY on the low left, EXCESS on the high right, balanced on SELF.)*

FIGURE 11-3

*Making Changes* 156

The id is that part of human consciousness driven to seek gratification and pleasure. The superego responds to social pressures. The ego modifies the demands of the id with the superego's considerations of the external world.

Freud's balancing point is what I call self, the fundamental agent of change. We are all capable of losing our balance from time to time. I hold a private theory that we can all be seduced by a conveyor belt full of temptations in life such as power, money, control, chemicals, attachments, and even qualities and achievements. When we focus too much on that conveyor belt or something on it, we can tip too far in favor of external concerns and find our internal lives undervalued and empty.

As we learned in Chapter One, we uncover evidence of excess and deficiency when we take the time to read the message of our pain and respond accordingly. The self remains the constant guide during this investigation. It is the force of judgment throughout the stages of childhood and maturity, and abides our failures as well as our successes. Self does undergo change as growth and development, and is modified by our interactions with the external environment. Self recycles experience with newfound revelation. We engage in a mental process of placing value on our thoughts and actions and on those of people around us. Then we decide to revalue in the light of changing reality. This is the process of selfing.

So, whenever a client tells me that she doesn't know herself, or, sadder yet, that she has no self, I explain that each person has a self and the ability to know it. Evidence of self exists in thoughts, feelings, and actions. Therefore, the task of selfing includes making statements that define and detail the individual's purpose and passions. Writing statements of your individual preferences outlines your self. It's as if you rubbed a pencil over a piece of blank paper that has the faintest impression of previously written words. With the right amount of pressure, the shading from the pencil lead will reveal what was written before.

People often come to know others indirectly. Think of the writers you know through their books, the musicians you know

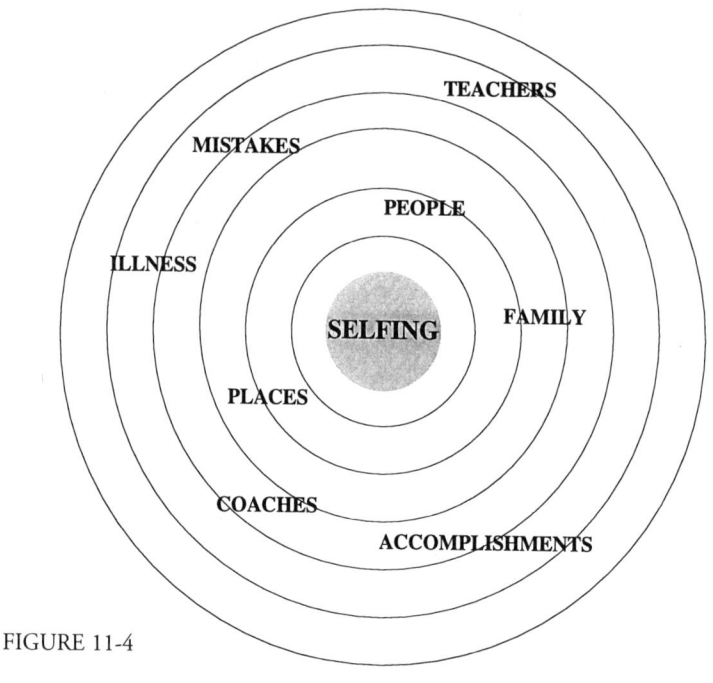

FIGURE 11-4

[Concentric circles diagram with SELFING at center, surrounded by rings labeled: PEOPLE, PLACES, FAMILY, COACHES, ACCOMPLISHMENTS, MISTAKES, ILLNESS, TEACHERS]

through their music, or the movie or television actors you know through their performances. For a more common example, think about someone at the office. Even though you may not have a close relationship, there are certain things you know about that person. Clues to an individual's inner self will appear on his or her desk. Does the person have a coffee cup that says World's Greatest Dad? Does she keep a jar full of perfectly sharpened pencils, or use a pen with her name etched on the barrel? Does he wear suspenders? Does she wear her high heels only in the office and change into Reeboks the moment the clock strikes four? Does she tell amusing stories about the difficulties of riding the bus? Does he laugh at his mistakes, or become withdrawn and sullen at the slightest criticism?

These are examples of preferences expressed in thoughts,

feelings, and actions. They are traces of self. Just as grief is an expression of the value of what once was, the choices we make express the value of what is and what will be. We say: This is important to me.

## Getting Practical
### Exercise One: Mining Mistakes

Besides the tasks associated with defining purpose and passion, selfing includes mining past mistakes in order to make lessons useful. Everyone makes mistakes. The selfing tasks allow a reevalu-

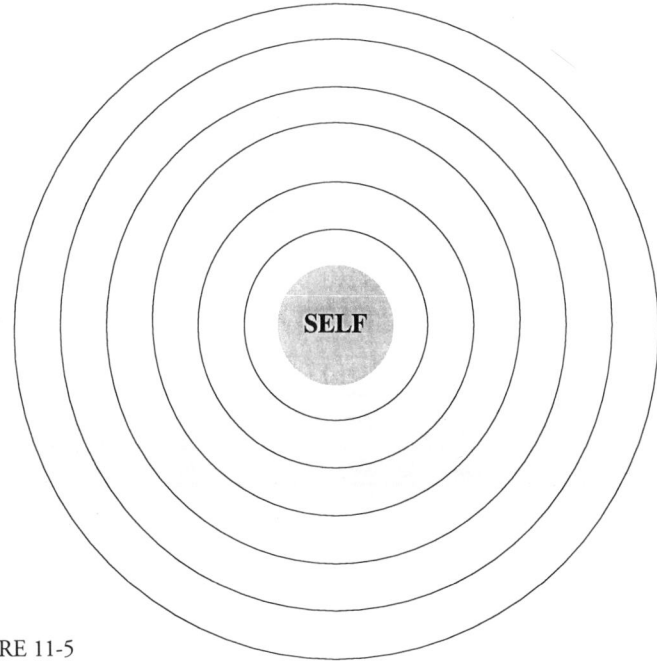

FIGURE 11-5

ation of the cause of the mistake. Whether the error occurred because of a lack of attention, knowledge, concern, or time, a lesson is there to learn. By mining our mistakes, we avoid repeating them in the future. Extracting what is of value involves examining the source of misjudgment, investigating its cause, and analyzing the relevant circumstances occurring at the time. It is a faulty belief to expect no mistakes to be made. We can adjust and correct future mistakes by acknowledging our mistakes and becoming aware of how they happen with an eye toward avoiding their repetition.

Revising cognitive behavioral responses based on the careful examination of past errors is a significant way of learning. Allowing past mistakes to recur promotes optional suffering, and repeating the same mistakes does not show good practice or good selfing.

Missing the mark and falling short of what we intend is a universal experience. This is why we have the capacity for hindsight.

As in all CBT exercises, the past exists only as a source of information. There is no value in reliving old miseries in hopes of changing the outcome. Don't dwell on what has been done; bring forward the experiences that will assist the change process from here on.

The next time you make a mistake, mine it. Dig around the construction of how it came to be in the first place.

## Exercise Two: Journey

Referring to Figure 11-5 on the previous page as an example, indicate the events, people, places, etc., you have experienced in your life cycle.

# Recycling

# 12
## RECYCLING

> *The power of the world always works in circles, and everything tries to be round.*
>
> —Black Elk

There is a revolution happening. We are doing the work of becoming ourselves. This personal revolution is one of self evolving into self. It's a contemporary recycling of self by integrating our experiences, mistakes, beliefs, feelings, thoughts and behaviors, taking whatever life hands us. We create the recycled self intentionally, changing the mind/body/spirit self in the present moment while still remaining connected to both the past and the future. This recycling is the work of CBT as developed in this book: learning from and deliberately using your life experience instead of mindlessly accumulating or being battered by whatever comes.

Robert Pirsig, author of *Zen and the Art of Motorcycle Maintenance*, begins his book by saying, "The real cycle you're working on is the cycle called yourself." Consequently, cycling never stops. No matter who you are or what you do, cycling continues as perpetual change. It is the way of life. Each of us is in a mini cycle, a part of the larger life cycle that is changing constantly.

I borrow from the nuances of the word revolution to talk about cycling and recycling. To revolve means to "move in a circular path or curved orbit, to rotate or recur periodically, or to turn around." Revolution initially was a word used by astrologers to refer to the motion of planets moving through space. In historical movements such as the Russian, Chinese, and Cuban revolutions, the meaning expanded to include the overthrow of tyrants and entrenched systems that didn't work. During the French Revolution, the term expanded further to imply belief in a new principle.

I borrow from all these meanings to discuss change as repeating cycles. The self moves through time and space experiencing pain and disruption, exploring the unknown and the new. Change involves expanding the possible, adapting from the past, weeding out what doesn't work. It is reusing the old canvas in the practice of pentimento, adjusting what you've done already, and changing the form of the familiar. Change is recycling all you are as part of the growth process.

Change is constant. It has no concern for whether we are aware of it, whether we seek it or shun it, or whether we adapt well or poorly. Change is as essential to life as the air we breathe. In fact, breathing illustrates this idea at a basic level. Breathing is a cycle of exchange. You can't just keep breathing out; neither can you only breathe in. Oxygen and carbon dioxide must exchange for life to continue. Just as each of us does our own breathing, each of us does our own knowing. Knowledge acquired through tested, lived experience is knowledge on which you can depend. True knowledge may involve discarding what you were taught is true. It may mean weeding out what doesn't match with your self now. When you allow time to pass and see results, which allows for hindsight, you gain a kind of knowing that can eventually transform into wisdom.

The fear that you will never get through unexpected change can be paralyzing. However, expecting that change will follow predictable cycles can help make it less disorienting. If you have a model to use as a road map, you can move through the cycle with some awareness.

Nature provides some examples of this predictability. The truest measure of time is in cycles. Natural time is marked by the sun rising and moving through the sky day after day, season after season, year after year. Women have intimate experience of the rhythm of cycles in the having-losing-having again of menstruation. Other cycles include: learning-unlearning-relearning; weeding out-evaluating usefulness-reusing; and losing-grieving-recovering from the loss. We develop a form of wisdom as we experience that these cycles change according to a predictable pattern.

Recycling is a metaphor for the way continuous change works in CBT. Change does not occur in a vacuum. It uses and reuses the material of the self, incorporating both useful and some useless parts. As the process continues, fewer useless parts are recycled.

Recycling as a part of personal change makes sense. It is difficult to move through the twelve steps of the cycle. Since the activities remain the same, we improve by studying our plans and seeing how we have finished. It's important to continue using what works and is reusable. Recycling saves energy, time, and money. Habits are especially economical. Think about exercise, for example. When you have a habit of regular exercise, you're in the practice of it. Think of all the debating, deciding, and negotiating you save yourself. You're on a schedule and you follow it. If you miss a time or two, the power of the habit will cause you to consider what happened, revise, and get back on schedule.

The self is the constant in the process of change. It holds all the experiential information of life. You must work with the information that is cycled into you. Authentic change occurs when our three primary parts (body/mind/soul) are working together harmoniously. This change model I teach is an evolved problem-solving method. It offers tools people can use to respond to change as whole, integrated beings. This model of planned change serves as a road map for going places you haven't been before. By using the model, you harness your powers of reason, body, and spirit to reduce the stress of change. It's always good to have some signs to advise you of the condition of the road ahead. Knowing what is coming can help you maneuver the curves. Using this model, you also practice counting on yourself.

> **To be truly ethical,
> you need to
> keep promises to yourself.**

FIGURE 12-2

What you say you want to do or be comes from inside yourself. Matching what is inside with what you present outside is integrity. Maintaining this integrity through change can be difficult because you are in unknown territory. The process of change takes you to places you've never been before and confronts you with the question of how to be there.

Writing is better than merely thinking as you recycle personal experience during this transition. To almost everyone, writing is a more serious act than speaking. Written words have a truth and permanence we don't find in speech alone. Knowledge is power. Telling the truth, your truth, is a good way of keeping promises to yourself.

This integrity and this truthfulness are the basis of personal ethics. If I am not true to my word, then who on earth can I trust? The act of writing your intentions increases the odds that you will follow them. Writing your intentions on paper is a commitment. I use writing to keep myself accountable to myself, to live honestly, to avoid energy dissipation, to honor my limitations, and to live on purpose.

Take a moment to reflect on promises you've made to yourself during the changes you're facing now, and jot them down. For example, I promise I'll recognize when I need help, and ask for it before I panic.

The map for responding to change leads from acknowledging through accepting to accommodating. The twelve steps through these changes remind us of the seasons of change, grounding us in the cycle of nature of which we are part.

Questioning, hurting, struggling, and clarifying illuminate what is out of balance so we can identify the pain. These steps help us acknowledge what is. The first attempts to fix the problem may not be effective. We need to look again to see the dynamics more clearly, stating the problem so we can solve it. Problems are not solved at the level they were created; we must evaluate the roles of our behaviors, internal messages, habits, rigid attitudes, and paralyzed thinking. When you know what and how you contribute to the problem, you'll know better how to contribute to the solution. This is acknowledging.

Accepting involves working through feelings and attachments, and then redirecting energy toward a new way of being with yourself. Claiming, releasing, and redefining are ongoing processes. Claiming is both accepting that you can't have something both ways and acknowledging anticipated losses. Releasing is acknowledging the reality of the facts as they are and letting go of that which you cannot control. Redirecting is then moving into the unknown and asking what happens now?

Accommodating is planning, choosing, practicing and selfing considering new insights and awareness of what you need. In planning and choosing, you use mental clarity to define a goal that you can achieve.

Practicing is living the way you say you want to live. It is reusing what you have learned that works and disposing of what is not useful. In selfing, you intentionally apply the sum of your identity and experience—your individuality—to whatever faces you in life, chosen or not. The difficult part about change is that we often don't know what we have to face until it's before us.

Recycling is repeating the same steps through change after change. The content changes, but the form remains the same. We cycle and recycle, discard and use what's useable again. We gather, reconsider, and reintegrate information. The same self evolves through life events, from birth to death, developing skill and wisdom through change.

After clients have finished a cycle, I often ask them to review what has happened during their change process. Let's do that now with the three people we have been following.

*Marie's grief process was very slow. It took more than two years for her to reorient herself to her life. Moving through pain, owning her deep losses, and redefining her identity as a seventy-year-old single woman was extremely difficult. At times she thought she would not* recover. *Five years later, when her brother died, she was present with his family to comfort and grieve. She knew how to use the multiple losses in her life as a source of strength. Her final reflection on pain was that it made her more compassionate.*

*When her new partner left her, Debbie realized she had a lot to learn. She felt secure in her new decisions, but realized she was disconnected from her deeper self. She had been through a great deal of pain. She resolved to approach new relationships differently. She began to manage the multiple roles that consumed her time and energy more effectively so she could spend more time in solitude and reflection. She began using what she had learned from the painful changes in her self.*

Being stuck in anger and resentment almost derailed Larry. His identification with one aspect of his personality had resulted in hopelessness when the reorganization of his company challenged his identity. When he was able to separate his value as a person from his demotion, he recovered his drive and channeled it into generating a more balanced perspective which included family, leisure, work and health. The new information he collected helped in changing his point of view—primarily, his perception of himself. He shared his new thoughts about balancing work with his brother, hoping to help him avoid some of the same patterns.

## Getting Practical
### Exercise One: Stress Smarts

You don't need to be overwhelmed with guidelines to effectively manage the stress of change. Working with my clients, I've found six categories that cover the essentials of stress management. I call them Stress Smarts. Like having a basic toolbox at home containing a few essential items, having some facility with each of these Stress Smarts is adequate to manage stress.

1. ***Think Differently.*** Thinking differently includes mental flossing. What do you control? Over what have you

limited control? What can you not control? Creative alternative thinking is certainly part of shifting perception. Changing our assessments and perceptions is the most effective stress tool I know. Doing so allows us to reframe the stress. Thinking is handy, immediate, and difficult to carry off. Build up stress immunity (mental and emotional immunity) by shifting shoulds, oughts, musts, and demands into alternative thinking.

2. *Physical Exercise.* Work physical exercise into your schedule no matter what. Do some exercise that fits you, your hairstyle, and your lifestyle.

3. *Self-Expression.* Self expression can be creative expression: dancing, art, writing letters, listening to music that matches your mood, building things, cleaning the house, cooking—the list is endless. It can be "telling it the way it is" to someone before you begin problem solving. Talking is by far the most underestimated stress management tool. It is free and usually available. Start there.

4. *Meditation.* Meditation includes care and nurturing of the soul. Put on your favorite music and sing along or dance around the house. Stay awake when you're awake. That means look around, notice, observe, and use all your senses.

5. *Nurturing.* Hot tea, hot baths, and hot love can all be part of nurturing yourself. Do things for yourself that compensate for what you do with most of your primary time and energy. Read good books and new magazines, light candles and enjoy chocolate. Again, the list is endless. Keep a list of comforts with you.

6. *Action.* Take action regarding the source of your stress. Quit or start leaving if that's what is necessary. Bite down hard on life. Stop doing what isn't working. You

may need to speak up, set limits, or perhaps lower your standards. The first five Stress Smarts address how you experience stress. The sixth urges action regarding the source of stress. We all need some skill in all the categories.

### EXERCISE TWO: THE ORIGINS OF UNHAPPINESS

Since paralyzed thinking is a sure trap, cite some examples of either-or-ism so you see the subtlety. Let those who choose to live in black and white suffer the loss of Technicolor.

### EXERCISE THREE: KEEPING YOUR REGRET LIST SHORT

A good way to keep your regret list short is by naming your regrets. A regret is something you think of with a sense of loss. It's something about which you feel sorrow or distress. It can be a mistake or a wrong you would not want to repeat. List what you consider regrets so that you can avoid recurrences. Comment on what makes each item on your list regrettable for you.

### EXERCISE FOUR: "PERFORMANCE"

Review. In a very free style, review the last twenty-four hours. Begin with this time yesterday. Jot words and phrases recounting how you spent your time. Mentally walk yourself through your last twenty-four hours, quickly and briefly listing what you did. Pay attention to your alone time, your morning and evening rituals, to whom you talked, phone calls, and meals. Don't leave out the ten minutes you read the funnies or slathered peanut butter on the toasted English muffin. The five minutes you browsed at Sherman's bakery while you decided between a raisin oatmeal or a chocolate chip cookie counts, too.

After you've filled pages with your activities, read through your account. Circle what you want to do more of, box what you want to do less of, and cross out what you don't want at all.

Finally, after reviewing your last twenty-four hours in this manner, complete the following sentence with any revelations you have. Write your first, second, and third thoughts.

*What I am aware of...*

_____
_____
_____

This is the end of the last chapter, but don't think it stops here. It just starts over in a different cycle.

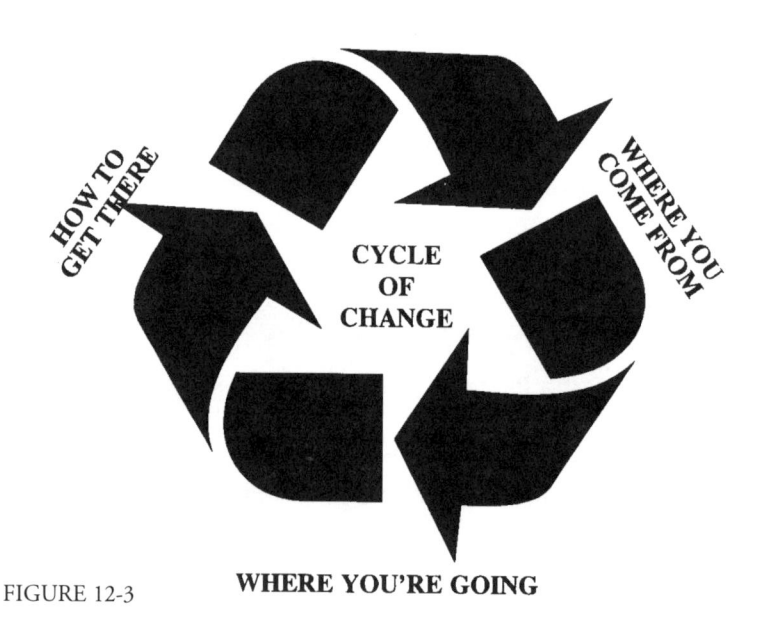

FIGURE 12-3

**CYCLE OF CHANGE**

**WHERE YOU COME FROM**

**HOW TO GET THERE**

**WHERE YOU'RE GOING**

# CONCLUSION

*C*hanging is life work that involves mind, body, and soul. It is learning, unlearning, and relearning.

The one-size-fits-all map for change that has been presented in this book works with both wanted and unwanted changes. But the map is not the journey, as the menu is not the meal. The journey is living, breathing, huffing-and-puffing-standing-on-your-own-two-feet-putting-one-foot-in-front-of-the other, in your own name and on your own behalf.

The benefit of practicing the way of change we've discussed is that you come to count on two things for certain: You can trust yourself and the cycle of change as things that are constant, and experience with the cycle builds trust in your ability to deal with change.

To sum up the change process, I would say:

1. Pain is an unavoidable part of life. It is a signal from our mind/body/spirit being that something is out of balance.
2. Questioning pain helps us to determine whether the pain is optional or necessary, and this is important because depending on the answer, different remedies and comfort measures apply.
3. Resistance is the common obstacle in dealing with change. Instead of confronting change, we try to strategize around and through it.
4. We can use mental flossing to rid ourselves of bad math, faulty beliefs, and emotional confusion. We can

seek the truth that is reality in order to be more accurately focused on clarifying what is changeable and what is not.

5. Claiming is an important piece of selfing. Claiming is so real that it has physical effects. It is knowing viscerally—by stomach-tightening and heart-pounding, that I am claiming the experience of my reality for what it is, rather than what I've been told it's supposed to be. My gut feelings indicate an acceptance of these truths of my experience.

    Our emotional stirrings tell us that things aren't going to remain the same. Claiming is mind/body/spirit positioning itself to risk releasing the known for the unknown. In other words, "When I choose to stop X, I start Y." Something's got to go. We need to claim our experiences as our own, for what they are rather than what they're supposed to be.

6. Releasing is the turning point of change, and the essence of releasing is letting go. It is both the decision to exchange this for that and the process of letting go. It includes, as I have said throughout this book, the actual act of revaluing: leaving instead of staying, letting go instead of clinging, living instead of dying. It is the activity that frees us to move on.

7. Redirecting involves refocusing your mental, physical and emotional energy—primarily your energy recently made available from letting go. When I release looking at past, for instance, I can look to now and to the future. Energy is neither created nor destroyed; it is transformed.

8. A goal without a plan is a wish. Planning is gathering and sifting through options, and redirecting our mental, physical and spiritual patterns occurs with specific, sequential steps in the direction we choose.
9. Choosing is the decision point. You say to yourself, Here's what I'm going to think and do so that, in time, I'll feel better. Choosing is similar to releasing, in that choosing is an act of decision, but you are aware of the many activities that support the choice (i.e., a choice to have a child is full of thousands of other choices).
10. We reinforce our new choices by practicing, and we need to practice whether we feel like it or not. We need to practice working through kinks and around roadblocks, come rain or come shine. We must be persistent, because practicing supports the choice on a daily basis.
11. Selfing is the steady insertion of me, such as I am, into my world. On a daily basis, I'm Colleening.
    Self is an entity plus the ongoing process of directing myself to be me in my style of being.
12. Recycling includes: 1) Reducing what isn't helpful or doesn't work. 2) Reusing what does work in keeping your mind/body/spirit in balance. 3) Remembering your pain and learning from it, in an effort to lessen mindless repetition of it. 4) Revising your map when you veer off course. 5) Rewarding yourself! 6) Renewing yourself regularly.

Remember, we are mind/body/spirit beings—as indivisible as a bubble. Be careful not to miss any part.

# ABOUT THE AUTHOR

*J*. Colleen Breen is an educator, consultant, and psychotherapist. For the past ten years she has been practicing Cognitive Behavioral Psychotherapy at Fairview Riverside Medical Center's Stress and Depression Management Center in Minneapolis, MN. She also has created Breen InnerPrizes, a consulting service dedicated to helping people deal with change.